The missing piece to improving your life is letting go of tension. Tension not only makes you unhappy, it keeps you stuck in your unhappiness. When you're tense you tend to do what's familiar and wrong instead of what's new and right.

This book takes a new approach to self-help. You don't have to work harder to improve your life. You will improve your life by letting go of the tension that's getting in your way.

There are three parts to the book. One – you'll learn how tension causes unhappiness and how it is an obstacle to change. Two – you'll learn a powerful technique to reduce your tension. Three – you'll learn how to apply that technique to improve specific areas of your life quickly.

Dr. Melemis learned the importance of relaxation after being diagnosed with cancer while in medical school. In the past 20 years he has taught the relaxation technique in this book, and has seen how it has improved people's lives. Read a clear step-by-step explanation of how and why relaxation works.

Reduce your anxieties and fears. Enjoy better relationships. Let go of resentments. Improve your self-esteem. Relieve depression. It's that one simple idea that can transform your life.

PRAISE FOR
Make Room for Happiness

This book is so clearly and beautifully crafted that just reading it reduces tension. Dr. Melemis has taken a complex subject and distilled it into pure therapeutic magic. Put simply: this book will heal you.

– **Hugh Prather**, author of *Notes to Myself*

This book could prove very beneficial to many people. I especially like the distinction between stress and tension and the clear instructions on how to engage in the various practices of relaxation.

– **Thupten Jinpa**, official translator to
the **Dalai Lama**

MAKE ROOM
for
HAPPINESS

12 Ways to Improve Your Life
By Letting Go *of* Tension.
Better Health, Self-Esteem, and
Relationships

STEVEN M. MELEMIS Ph.D. M.D.

Modern Therapies
Toronto

Library and Archives Canada Cataloguing in Publication

Melemis, Steven M. (Steven Michael), 1952-
    Make room for happiness : 12 ways to improve your life by letting go of tension : better health, self-esteem and relationships / Steven M. Melemis.

Includes bibliographical references and index.
ISBN 978-1-897572-17-7 (pbk.).--ISBN 978-1-897572-18-4 (bound)

    1. Stress (Psychology). 2. Happiness. 3. Stress management.
4. Self-actualization (Psychology). I. Title.
BF575.S75.M46 2008   155.9'042   C2008-902372-2

Editing: Ricki Ewings and Julia Kiessling
Copy editing and indexing: Wendy Thomas
Cover design: Catherine McKenny
Interior layout: Olena Sullivan
Publishing Consultant: Ellen Reid
Author's photo: Edward Gajdel
Printed in the United States

Contents

1.

INTRODUCTION

The pursuit of happiness involves three things. You have to identify what makes you unhappy, let it go, and learn the things that make you happy. This book will help you with all three steps.

The main idea of the book is that tension is an obstacle to each step in the pursuit of happiness. Tension is an obstacle because when you're tense it's hard to let go of your old habits to make room for change. Have you ever read a self-help book and then repeated the same mistakes? When you're tense you tend to repeat what's familiar and wrong instead of doing what's new and right.

You will learn three important lessons in this book. One – you'll learn how tension causes unhappiness and how it is an obstacle to change. Two – you'll learn a simple and powerful technique to reduce your tension. Three – you'll learn how to apply that technique to improve specific areas of your life quickly.

You will learn how to improve your self-esteem, have better relationships, improve your health, reduce anxiety, and get more out of life by letting go of your tension.

This book takes the opposite approach of most self-help books. You don't have to work harder to find happiness – instead you will find happiness by letting go of the tension that's getting in your way. It's that one simple idea that can transform your life.

I'd like to tell you a little about the motivation behind this book before we get started. I'm a doctor who has been practicing medicine for over twenty years. Many of my patients are doctors, lawyers, and nurses who have been referred to me by their professional associations, usually because they've run into trouble with depression or substance abuse. I also give a weekly lecture at a local hospital, and I've discovered that most people's problems are the same no matter what their job or how much money they make.

Every day I see how tension ruins people's lives. People want better relationships, but can't let go of the resentments and fears that are getting in their way. People want to improve their self-esteem, but can't let go of the doubts that are defeating them. People are dying of heart attacks at ever younger ages. This is a wake-up call to the destructive effects of tension and a strategy for overcoming them.

After hearing enough stories from my patients, I began to see a pattern. Everybody wanted to improve their life, but most people kept on repeating the same mistakes. The question was why. These people were intelligent, hardworking self-starters. They were successful in every other aspect of their life. But when it came to changing their life, they were stuck. Most of them had read self-help books or had gone to therapy. They knew their issues. But they kept on repeating the same mistakes.

My experience led me to what I call my "laws of happiness." My first law is the inescapable conclusion that knowledge alone does not help people change or find happiness. Knowledge doesn't prevent people from repeating the same mistakes. The standard approach to self-help is to give people more information. Show them what they're doing wrong, and tell them what they should do instead, believing that will help them change. But that's usually the easy part. Most people already know what they're doing wrong.

My second law took a little longer to figure out. But eventually I realized that tension was the main negative factor in my patients' lives. When they were tense, their relationships suffered. When they were tense, their depression deepened. When they were tense, their self-esteem was more vulnerable. Tension affects almost every aspect of life. Many of my patients didn't know how to reduce their tension, and the few who did know how to relax were too busy to relax. Therefore my second law of happiness is that tension is the biggest preventable cause of unhappiness.

Once I realized the importance of tension, I came to my third law. Tension is the main obstacle to change. Tension not only makes people unhappy, it keeps them stuck in their unhappiness by making it hard to change. When people are tense, they tend to do what's familiar and wrong instead of what's new and right. When they're tense, they find it hard to let go of their egos and fears to make room for change.

My final law is that reducing tension will improve your life and help you change your life. Letting go of tension is the missing piece of how you change your life. Think of it this way. There are many coping skills that you need to be happy in life. If you learn them all but don't learn how to reduce your tension, you still won't be happy, because when you're tense you'll continue to repeat what's familiar and wrong. On the other hand, if you don't learn any new coping skills, but learn only one new skill – how to relax – you'll still be happier, because everything is easier when you're relaxed. If there is anything else you need to change in order to be happier, you'll see it more easily and deal with it more effectively when you're more relaxed.

If you follow the simple steps in this book, I'm confident that within a month you will begin to enjoy your life more. You'll be more relaxed and tolerant. Your relationships will improve and you'll be happier in life.

My Story

I'd also like to tell you about my own personal experience with tension. I first learned how to relax out of necessity. Two months after starting medical school, I was diagnosed with cancer. I was treated with surgery followed by months of radiation, and then the doctor told me that if I could survive the next five years I would be considered cured. I don't think I was consciously worried about dying, but the combination of that plus the stress of medical school eventually gave me an ulcer. I needed to learn to relax.

I'm a firm believer that doctors would be more empathetic if they had to go through at least one serious illness before graduation. We doctors are so busy that we sometimes forget to treat people with dignity. We forget that a disease doesn't just break a person's body, it breaks their spirit. And a person's spirit isn't repaired with drugs or surgery, but with caring.

When I developed my ulcer, the doctor gave me a barium X-ray, a bunch of pills, a pat on the back, and sent me home. I had questions I wanted to ask, but I could see from the look in his eyes that he had other patients to take care of.

So I went to the bookstore and got a few books on stress management. Unfortunately they weren't helpful because I quickly realized that stress was an integral part of my job. I couldn't manage my stress away. So I went back to the bookstore and bought a few books on relaxation. But I didn't find them helpful either, because they seemed mystical. I was supposed to imagine that I was a tranquil pond or a mountain. I was going into my medical exams with what felt like a brick of coal burning in my stomach. I needed results fast.

Eventually I pieced together the common elements in all the relaxation techniques I had read about and began to practice that. Once I found a technique that was simple to follow, I was amazed at how quickly I started to feel better. I've been practicing relaxation ever since. I'm embarrassed to admit that before I developed my ulcer I had never thought about relaxation.

I learned an important lesson reading those books. A patient wants solutions to his or her problems. Not necessarily quick solutions, but real solutions. I didn't want to read a lot of filler. I have tried to bring that philosophy into this book.

Surviving cancer was both terrifying and liberating. It taught me a valuable lesson that I should have known all along, which is that life is a precious gift. We are on this world for only a short time, and we shouldn't waste it.

After graduating from medical school, I set up my practice and began teaching mindbody relaxation to some of my patients. At first, I was worried that they might think I was too far out there. But many of them were kind enough to try relaxation, and most of them found it helpful. Over time, I became even more convinced that mindbody relaxation was the key to happiness and to changing one's life.

I began giving lectures on relaxation, and patients would come up to me afterward and ask me if there were any books on the subject that I could recommend. That's when I remembered the advice of Toni Morrison, who said, "If there's a book you really want to read, but it hasn't been written yet, then you must write it." I thought I would write a short, ten-page handout for my patients – and ended up writing this book.

It took eight years to finish the book. The first version was somewhere between a typical meditation book and the book that I really wanted to write. Once I had written the first version and got it out of my system, I sat down and realized that I needed a new way of talking about relaxation. I didn't want to just reach the people who were already interested in meditation. I wanted to reach the people who had never thought about relaxation, but who could benefit from it.

This book is based on my years of helping people improve their life. Most of them were initially skeptical about the importance of letting go of tension, but almost all of them eventually saw it as their most important coping skill. Sit back and enjoy yourself.

May this book bring you peace, happiness, and good health.

PART 1.
THE PROBLEM AND THE SOLUTION

2.
WHAT TENSION IS AND HOW IT CAUSES UNHAPPINESS

Tension is different from stress. Stress is what happens around you, and tension is what you feel. Stress is inevitable. If you have to go to work every day, if you have to deal with people, there's no getting around stress. On the other hand, you can do something about your tension.

The only way you can avoid stress is by avoiding life. Therefore this book will show you how to get more out of life by reducing your tension. If there *is* anything you can do about your stress, you'll be able to deal with it more effectively when you're more relaxed.

There are four basic causes of tension:

- Not being in the moment
- Resentments
- Fears
- Trying to control things you can't control

All forms of tension are a combination of those four basic causes. Guilt, for example, is a combination of dwelling on the past, resentment, and fear.

Not Being In the Moment

When you're not in the moment, you're either dwelling on the past or worrying about the future. You replay events from the past again and again, as if you're looking for a better ending. You know you're wasting your time, but sometimes you can't seem to stop yourself.

You tell yourself that you want to understand what happened, so that you won't let it happen again. But how many times do you have to go over the same thing? Most of the time you're just spinning your wheels. Understanding the past is an important part of change because it helps you understand how the past affects your present. But dwelling on the past beyond that point doesn't help you anymore. If anything it makes you more tense and resentful.

The time you spend worrying about the future is usually just as unproductive. You worry about things that will probably never happen. Has this ever happened to you? You have a big interview or meeting coming up and you completely throw yourself into it. You worry about it. You stay up late at night thinking about it, and then when the event finally arrives you're so exhausted or frazzled that you don't perform to your maximum ability.

Of course it's important that you prepare for the future. But there's a difference between preparing for the future and worrying about it. A big part of preparing for the future is being relaxed and in the moment when it arrives.

"When you're not in the moment, it feels like you're surviving life instead of living it."

The other way you're not in the moment is when you're in a rush to do many things at once, but don't enjoy what you do. You overbook your life thinking you can relax later, but the moment you finish one thing you rush to start the next. It feels like you're never doing enough. And the faster you work, the more frazzled you get, and the more work you take on. Tension creates a vicious cycle that leads to more tension. At the end of the day, you've accomplished a lot, but you're so exhausted that you can't enjoy what you've accomplished. When you're not in the moment, it feels like you're surviving life instead of living it.

In the moment is the only place you can be happy. In the moment is where you are when you're relaxed and having fun. In the moment is where you are when you're on holiday. It's one of the things that you like about being on holiday – the chance to slow down and enjoy the moment. We admire children for their ability to enjoy the moment. But most people probably spend less than a few minutes a day being in the moment. What percent of the day do you spend enjoying the moment?

"It seems that our life is all past and future, and that the present is nothing more than an infinitesimal hairline which divides them. From this comes the sensation of 'having no time,' of a world that hurries by so rapidly that it is gone before we can enjoy it. But through awakening to the instant, one sees that the reverse is true. It is rather the past and future which are the fleeting illusions, and the present which is eternally real."[1]
– Alan W. Watts (1915–1973)

Resentments

Resentments are always about people, and your deepest resentments are about the people closest to you. It has been said that resentments are like drinking poison and hoping that the other person will get hurt. The more you dwell on your resentments, the more you poison yourself, and the more the other person wins. The other person has long forgotten what happened between the two of you. They've moved on. But you're still poisoning yourself.

One thing I've learned from practicing medicine is that everyone has resentments, and everyone wastes time on fantasies of revenge. Part of the time you spend dwelling on the past, you're probably dwelling on your resentments. You fantasize about what you'll say to the other person and how they'll apologize. You practice your victory address. When I tell audiences, "Your deepest resentments are about the people closest to you," everyone looks around as if I've exposed a deep secret. Relax, we're all alike. Even someone as enlightened as the Dalai Lama admits, "We have all been responsible for countless ill deeds of body, speech, and mind, motivated by the desire to do harm."[2]

> **"We hold on to resentments as if they're precious possessions, instead of letting them go like the poison that they are."**

Resentments are a powerful poison. A small resentment in the morning has the power to spoil your whole day. A deep resentment from the past can upset you years later. You've probably met people who've held on to their resentments their whole life only to end up bitter old people. What do all those resentments accomplish? We hold on to resentments as if they're precious possessions, instead of letting them go like the poison they are.

How do you eliminate resentments? The answer is you can't completely eliminate them. Bad things happen. Life isn't fair. Letting go of tension doesn't mean you'll never be resentful again. Letting go of tension means that when something bad happens you can let go of your resentments quickly, which is the next best thing.

When you don't know how to let go of resentments, if something bad happens, you carry it with you for the rest of the day. You dwell on it. You brood over it. And by the end of the day you're carrying it with you. You gradually build layer upon layer of resentment until resentments are all you see. Letting go of your tension means that you can get on with your life quickly.

One of my patients told me a sad but funny story about resentments. Gerry's wake-up call that he was too resentful came when he was driving his son to baseball practice. Gerry had a great deal of road rage. One day, his six-year-old son who was sitting next to him in their car turned to Gerry and said, "We hate everybody in front of us, don't we, Dad?"

Judging others is a subtle form of resentment. Being judgmental is different from other resentments because it's so easy to justify. After all, your way of doing something is the right way and their way is wrong. And through some combination of ego that your way is better and frustration that they aren't following a better way, you end up becoming resentful. But no matter how right you might be, the result of being judgmental is still the same. You end up poisoning yourself. When you see the world as black and white, right or wrong, good or bad, you'll spend most of your time focused on what is wrong. One of the benefits of relaxation is that it helps you become less judgmental so that you have more time to enjoy your life.

"Before you embark on a journey of revenge, dig two graves."
– Confucius (551–479 BCE[3])

Fears

Fear is the most difficult cause of tension to recognize. What do you worry about the most? Most people would say fear of death or fear of failure. But if you were really honest with yourself, you'd probably say that you worry about being judged or criticized. You worry about what other people think about you. It affects everything you do, from what you say to what you wear.

Fear of criticism begins early with the criticism you receive growing up. You know what that sounds like. "Don't be silly." "Can't you do anything right?" "If you keep that up, you'll never amount to anything." "Don't be stupid." Everyone has heard those criticisms before. Small doses of destructive criticism are normal. Parents are doing the best they can, and nobody is perfect. But the more you're criticized, the more you begin to believe it, until eventually it damages your self-esteem. If you have fears you will probably have resentments too because most people subconsciously resent that which they fear.

**"The most common fear is the fear of
being judged or criticized."**

There is no easy antidote to criticism. Fear of criticism is hard to erase. Praise doesn't erase the sting of criticism. Being told you are loved does not undo being told you are stupid. "I love you, but don't be stupid." If you're like most people, you've probably heard both of those messages. The result is that you're probably an uncomfortable mix of self-confidence and low self-esteem. You're confident in some parts of your life, but frustrated by self-doubt in others.

Consider the case of Jennifer, a lawyer who grew up with an alcoholic father. Jennifer's dad was the nicest guy in the world when he was sober, but when he was drunk he was sarcastic. Jennifer can still remember his put-downs years later. The result is that no matter how successful she becomes, Jennifer feels like a fraud inside. On her worst days she can hear her father's voice criticizing her. Jennifer is successful and attractive, but she has been unable to end a long-term relationship with a married man. She worries that if she was in a real relationship with someone who could spend time with her, he would eventually discover that she was a fraud.

Trying to Control Things That You Can't Control

What do you try to control the most? The actions of other people. Of course, you know you can't control other people, but the more tense you are, the more you try. What do you do when you're standing in line? You probably try to control how fast the people ahead of you move. What do you do when you're driving? You probably try to control how fast the other drivers drive. They're either going too slow or too fast. Trying to control things that you can't control is a main source of frustration in life.

When you are tense, you blur the line between what happens around you and what you feel inside. It feels as if things are happening to you instead of happening around you. Therefore you try to control them. It feels like people are going out of their way to irritate you when you're tense. But when you're relaxed, you see things as simply happening, which makes it easier to let them go.

**"When you're tense, it feels as if things are
happening to you instead of happening around you.
Therefore you try to control them."**

Sounds are a good test of how controlling you are. You'll be distracted by all kinds of sounds when you try to relax. You'll be distracted by trucks driving by, kids playing, and people working outside. Those sounds will trigger all kinds of emotions, including resentments, fears, and the impulse to control.

The more tense you are, the more those simple sounds will feel like irritating noise, and your reaction to noise is to wish it away or to try to control it. You'll demonize the people making the noise. You'll think that they're being inconsiderate. You may even think that they enjoy disturbing you, even though they don't know you're there. I can assure you most people think like that.

How you deal with the few sounds beyond your control when you try to relax is how you deal with the many things beyond your control in the rest of your life. If you dwell on the details of the sound, you'll only make yourself more tense. If you demonize the people making the sounds, you'll end up poisoning yourself. You will only relax when you acknowledge that you make yourself tense. People make pilgrimages to India only to discover that they have to meditate over blaring car horns and rumbling traffic. The sounds aren't directed at you. They aren't meant to harm you. Let go of your desire to control the things you can't control, and save your energy for the things you can control.

The word that best describes the four causes of tension is "grasp." Don't grasp at the past or the future. Live in the moment. Let go of your resentments and fears by not grasping at them. They exist in the past and the future. Enjoy the moment.

There is a beautiful proverb about letting go by the eighth-century sage Santideva. He said, if you walk barefoot in the world, there are many sticks and stones that will hurt your feet. Can you cover the earth with leather so that it is soft wherever you go? Of course not. But you can cover your feet with leather, which amounts to the same thing and is easier to do.[4] Likewise there are many things in your life that you won't like. You can't control them all. But you let go of your desire to control them, which has the same effect and is better for you.

"Grant me the serenity to accept the things I cannot change,
The courage to change the things I can,
And the wisdom to know the difference."
– *The Serenity Prayer*

Layers of Tension

The four causes of tension build layers of tension, which combine to make you overreact to things. If you don't know how to let go of your tension, every day you'll add more layers of tension to the pile. Each layer of tension is connected with every other layer, so that one layer can trigger the other. For example, some little thing happens to you, and you overreact to it, not because of the little thing that just happened, but because of all the things it represents. Somebody bullies you or embarrasses you, and it reminds you of all the times you've been bullied or embarrassed in the past.

Consider your average day. You begin with a little resentment during your morning commute. If you don't let it go, the next resentment that comes along will build on top of the first. Once you have two resentments, you won't think of them as individual resentments. You'll just know that you're angry, and you won't even know why. If a third resentment comes along, you'll be on your way to taking your resentments home and having them affect your relationships. It's that easy. You probably have three resentments by the time you've had lunch. What chance do you have to be happy, if you don't let all that stuff go?

"I've never met anyone whose behavior wasn't affected by the fears and resentments they developed as a child."

Tension has deep roots. I've never met anyone whose behavior wasn't affected by the fears and resentments they developed as a child. When someone criticizes you or embarrasses you, you automatically remember how it felt to be criticized or embarrassed as a child. The more tense you are, the closer those layers of tension are to the surface and the more they distort your behavior. One of the reasons children smile so easily is because they have fewer layers of tension to make them unhappy.

Your layers of tension aren't pretty. When you try to relax, don't be surprised to find long-forgotten resentments, sitting next to lists of worries, mixed in with embarrassments, all fueled by guilt, fear, regret, and hatred. The more you look at your tension, the more you'll wonder why it's still renting space in your head. But only by recognizing your tension can you let it go. And only by letting it go can you change your life.

Relaxation changes the way you see the world. Tension isn't about what happens around you – it's about what you carry inside. You are the cause of your tension. And you have the ability to let it go.

"There are four basic causes of tension: not being in the moment, resentments, fears, and trying to control things you can't control."

3.
How to Improve Your Life By Letting Go of Tension

The previous chapter showed you how tension causes unhappiness. In this chapter you'll learn how tension keeps you trapped in your unhappiness, and how letting go of tension can improve your life.

The Process of Self-Change

Self-change and the pursuit of happiness involve three steps:

- Identify how you make yourself unhappy.
- Let go of those negative behaviors.
- Learn positive behaviors in their place.

Happiness is an inside job. Before you look at external things to change in your life, have a look at yourself. There's no doubt that external factors are an important part of happiness. But some external factors you cannot change, and the external factors that are easy to change are the ones that don't contribute much to your long-term happiness.

If you don't change who you are, any external changes you make will usually be nice for a while, but then you'll quickly go back to feeling the way you did before. This chapter looks at how letting go of tension will change your life from the inside out.

Identify What Is Getting in Your Way

When you're tense, you tend to focus on the external causes of your unhappiness and blame other people for your problems. It's your boss, or your spouse, or the system that are making you unhappy, but it's hard to step back to see how you make yourself unhappy.

When you're relaxed it's easier to let down your guard and see how you contribute to your unhappiness. Do you dwell on the past or worry about the future instead of enjoying the moment. Do you carry old resentments and fears that get in the way of your relationships? Do your fears make you overreact to little things? It's hard to see yourself at the best of times, but it's especially hard to see yourself when you're tense.

"Relaxation helps you see yourself because it is a reflection of your life."

Relaxation helps you see yourself because it is a reflection of your life. The thoughts that are obstacles to your happiness in life are the thoughts that will make you tense when you try to relax. The techniques that you use to let go of your tension when you try to relax are the techniques you will use to be happier in life.

If resentments are a major source of unhappiness in your life, then you'll probably dwell on your resentments as you try to relax. If fears are interfering with your life, you'll probably be distracted by your fears as you try to relax. If you rush through your life and forget to enjoy the moment, you'll probably rush through your relaxation.

Those are the issues that most people need to change in order to be happy. But you'll only see them when you're relaxed. (You'll learn more about how to improve your self-esteem in Chapter 13, and how to improve your relationships in Chapter 16.)

Tension may be the only thing you need to change in your life. Tension blinds you to what you really have. Maybe your tension is preventing you from appreciating the positive things that you have in your life. It's hard to appreciate your life when you're rushing through it. It's hard to appreciate your relationships when you hold on to old resentments. Maybe there is nothing else that you need to change. Maybe your tension is turning a perfectly good life into a perfectly miserable one.

If there are any external factors that you need to change, you'll see them more clearly and deal with them more effectively when you're relaxed.

"He who knows other men is clever; he who knows himself is wise. He who overcomes others is strong; he who overcomes himself is mighty."[5]
– *Lao-Tzu (sixth century BCE)*

Let Go of Your Negative Behaviors

This is where letting go of tension helps the most. The second step in the pursuit of happiness is making room for change. It's letting go of your negative behaviors and traits so that you can be open to change. Most people try to change their life by focusing on the first step of self-change. They try to identify why they're unhappy, thinking that should lead to change. But that's usually the easy part.

What you need to know as far as happiness is concerned you probably already know, and what you need to change you've probably already figured out. Life is simple. It's tension that makes it complicated. Have you ever asked yourself, "How could I be so smart but do such stupid things?" That's because tension keeps you stuck in your old habits.

Knowing what you need to change isn't the same as change. Most people continue to focus on the first step of change and dwell on why they're unhappy. They go over the same disappointments, frustrations, and resentments. They tell themselves, they need to figure out every last detail of what went wrong so that they'll be ready next time. But if dwelling on why you're unhappy was such a great idea, you'd be happy by now. Letting go of your tension opens the door to change.

"If dwelling on why you're unhappy was such a great idea, you'd be happy by now."

When you're tense, you tend to do what's familiar and wrong instead of what's new and right. This is reason that tension is an obstacle to change, and why letting go of tension makes room for change. It helps you let go of your ego and fears so that you can be open to change. It helps you focus on improving the present instead of repeating the past. It makes you open to learning something new and trying something new. Change isn't just about what you learn, it's also about what you let go.

🍃 🍃 🍃

"To gain knowledge, add something every day.
To gain wisdom, let go of something every day."[6]
– Lao-Tzu (sixth century BCE)

Develop Positive Behaviors

Once you've identified what you need to change, and let it go, the final step in the process of self-change is learning healthier behaviors. Perhaps you want to be more understanding and compassionate. Perhaps you want to enjoy the little things in life and be more in the moment. Most people feel that those qualities would improve their life and their relationships. But how do you cultivate those qualities in this stressful world? This book doesn't just say you must be more understanding or more in the moment. It gives you a map of how to get there.

The process of relaxation is a map of how to cultivate healthy behaviors. Relaxation helps you bring positive qualities into your life because you practice those positive behaviors during your relaxation session. During a relaxation session you practice being free of resentments so that you can reproduce that feeling later. You practice being in the moment so that you can be in the moment during the rest of your day. Relaxation helps you replace resentments and fears with positive emotions like joy and enthusiasm. Those are the skills that bring real happiness.?

> **"Letting go of tension is the missing piece of how you change your life."**

Think of it this way. There are many coping skills that you need to be happy in life. If you learn them all but don't learn how to relax, you still won't be happy, because when you're tense you'll continue to repeat what's familiar and wrong. On the other hand, if you don't learn any new coping skills, but learn only one new skill – how to relax – you'll still be happier, because everything is easier when you're relaxed. Letting go of tension is the missing piece of how you change your life.

All change is difficult, even good change. You've repeated your old habits thousands of times. You'll have to repeat your new habits a few hundred times before they start to feel natural. Relaxation is that practice. You practice being relaxed, compassionate, happy, and in the moment so that you can bring those positive qualities into your life.

The Purpose of Life

"I believe that the very purpose of our life is to seek happiness.…
One begins by identifying those factors which lead to happiness
and those which lead to suffering. Having done this, one then sets
about gradually eliminating those factors which lead to suffering
and cultivating those which lead to happiness." [7]
– The Dalai Lama

Relaxation serves the purpose of life. It helps you identify the factors that make you unhappy, let them go, and learn something better in their place. It's that one simple idea that can transform your life.

"When you're tense you tend to do what's familiar and wrong instead of what's new and right."

PART 2.
HOW TO REDUCE YOUR TENSION

4.
USE YOUR BODY TO RELAX YOUR MIND

It's hard to relax by thinking you should relax. The more you try to relax by thinking about it, the more tense you become. It's like chasing your tail. In this chapter you'll learn how to avoid that trap. You will learn a simple technique that you can use to relax and let go of your anxiety in every situation.

The Key to Relaxation

The key to relaxation is – don't try to relax your mind. You will relax your mind by relaxing your body. Your mind and body are in constant communication, and if you relax your body your mind will follow.

To understand how that works, try this simple 60-second experiment. If you are sitting in a chair, rest both your feet comfortably on the ground. Imagine your feet and legs becoming heavy. Now mentally scan the soles of your feet, and focus on how each point feels where your soles touch the ground. It's important that you feel the soles of your feet instead of trying to visualize them. Do that for a few breaths before moving on.

Next, imagine your whole body becoming heavy and loose. Mentally scan the points where your body touches the chair and focus on feeling your seat and hips. Feel them. Don't try to visualize them. Feel yourself letting go and getting heavier with each breath. Do that for a few more breaths. Then read further.

If you did that simple experiment, you're already breathing more slowly and feeling more relaxed. It's that reliable. What's amazing is how quickly you can relax once you know how.

"Don't try to relax your mind. Relax your body and your mind will follow."

Mindbody Relaxation Techniques

Most relaxation techniques are based on the idea that if you relax your body, you will relax your mind. All these techniques belong to the general category of "mind-body techniques." There is a spectrum of mind-body techniques. At one end of the spectrum are simple techniques like going for a walk. When you go for a walk, it relaxes both your body and mind. The problem with going for a walk is that sometimes it works but sometimes it doesn't help you relax. It's not always reliable.

At the other end of the spectrum are structured techniques like the one you're about to learn. It's a simple and powerful technique that you can rely on to relax anywhere.

Mind-body techniques go by many different names, including mindfulness-based stress reduction and mindful meditation. I prefer the simple term "relaxation" because it says what you're trying to achieve. When I have to distinguish between the feeling of relaxation and the practice of relaxation, I'll use the term "mindbody relaxation." I think the mind and body are so connected that they shouldn't be separated by a hyphen.

An Overview of How to Relax

There are two components to mindbody relaxation:

1. Relax your muscles.
2. Become aware of your tension.

You begin by relaxing your muscles. Once your muscles are relaxed, your mind will begin to relax. Once your mind begins to relax, you'll be able to identify the underlying cause of tension that's preventing you from relaxing further. That underlying cause of tension will be some combination of not being in the moment, resentment, fear, or trying to control things you can't control. Once you're aware of that tension, name it. Naming your tension helps you recognize it more easily in the future. Then let go of that tension and complete the cycle by returning to your body and relaxing it further. The more times you go around the cycle, the more layers of tension you will let go, and the more relaxed you will be.

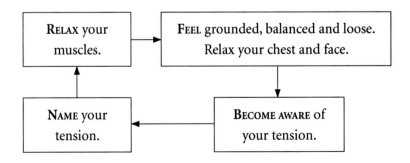

You have three main areas of tension in your body: the core muscles that control your posture, your chest muscles, and your face. In this chapter you'll learn how to relax your core muscles by becoming grounded, balanced, loose, and centered. In Chapter 5 you will learn how to relax your chest muscles. In Chapter 6 you will learn how to relax your face. Chapter 7 will show you how to stay focused by repeating a word or phrase. In Chapter 8 you'll learn how to become aware of your tension. Chapters 9 and 10 are about how relaxation works and feels. Chapter 11 deals with common problems in relaxation. And in Chapter 12 you'll learn how to put it all together.

Become Grounded, Balanced, and Loose

Relax your body by becoming grounded, balanced, loose, and centered. Those four qualities describe how it feels to be relaxed. They are true whether you are lying down, sitting, or standing. During a relaxation session you practice producing those four qualities so that you can reproduce them later. That's how it works. In this section you'll learn how to become grounded, balanced, and loose, and in the next section you'll learn how to become centered.

Feel the contact you make with the ground. When you're tense, your body doesn't rest comfortably on the ground. Your muscles lift you up slightly so that you're ready to fight or run. To become grounded, mentally scan the points where your body touches the ground and focus on how each point feels. When you feel each point, you become aware of the difference between the grounded and the ungrounded parts of your body, which helps you relax. During a relaxation session, ask yourself, "What part of my body is tense?" and it will help you see where you should focus.

You can relax by becoming grounded anywhere. If you're lying down, you can relax by scanning the contact your back makes with the ground. If you're sitting, standing, or walking, you can relax by mentally scanning the soles of your feet. When you're very tense, try focusing on a small area like your toes, and work your way out from there. If you focus on too large an area it's hard to maintain your focus.

Distribute your weight evenly. When you're tense, your body is leaning to one side or the other as if you're getting ready to run. You're literally on edge. It's impossible to feel relaxed when your muscles are working that hard to keep you on edge. You become balanced by imagining the four corners of your feet, or the four corners of your seat, and shifting your weight so that it's evenly distributed.

Loosen your muscles. You store a lot of tension in your shoulders, neck, and back, where it shows up as knotted muscles and backaches. Consciously try to relax your muscles. It helps to imagine them warming up and melting or lengthening as they relax. If you have a hard time loosening your muscles, try tensing them up first. That will give you a feel for what you're trying to undo.

The combination of becoming grounded, balanced, and loose helps to relax your core muscles and is the first step in relaxing your mind.

Become Centered

Being centered means that your focus is centered within you. When you're aware of your body and when you're grounded, balanced, and loose, you are centered. You turn your thoughts into your body and away from your tension. When you're tense, your thoughts are out there, focused on someone else or something else. Being centered helps you feel relaxed because you turn your thoughts away from your distractions.

**"To feel comfortable in your own skin, you have to
be in your own skin."**

To feel comfortable in your own skin, you have to be in your own skin. Stop every once in a while over the next few days, and see what you're focused on. You'll see that when you're tense, it's almost as if you're not aware of your body. You're too focused on someone or something else.

Being centered doesn't mean that you turn your back to the world, or that you're focused only on yourself. But if you took a series of snapshots of what you were focused on, you would see that when you were relaxed your focus turned inward from time to time. When you're tense, your focus was almost completely turned outward.

When you're distracted during a relaxation session, you can almost physically feel your center of focus move away from you as you focus on something else. When you're grounded, balanced, and loose you can physically feel your center of focus move back into your body, and as you do that you will feel yourself be more with the moment. Your body exists in the moment, and when you focus on it you connect with the moment.

A good way to monitor if you're centered during a relaxation session is to check what your eyes are doing. Most people like to relax with their eyes closed. When you're centered, your eyes will be soft and looking forward. When you're tense, your eyes will be looking off to the side, or following thoughts in your mind's eye. They'll be scanning your surroundings looking for threats. Your eyes are a measure of how hypervigilant you are and also how relaxed and centered you are.

**"Your body exists in the moment, and when you
focus on it you connect with the moment."**

One of my favorite techniques for becoming centered is a visualization technique that's often taught to cancer patients. Sit quietly and imagine your body filling up with white light. It's an easy technique to learn, and patients find that they can quickly use it to become centered and relaxed. It helps cancer patients overcome the nausea of radiation or chemotherapy. It applies here because when you imagine your body radiating white light, you have to turn your focus inward, which means you have to turn your thoughts away from your tension. There is a subtle point to this technique, which is, don't try to visualize white light. Visualize the white light coming from within your body. I especially like this technique because you can combine it with other techniques.

Basic Relaxation Tips

There are three basic relaxation postures. You can relax lying down, sitting on the floor, or sitting in a chair. Sitting cross-legged is probably the best known relaxation posture, but also the most difficult. No one posture is any better at relaxing than any other. Lying down is a traditional meditation posture that Zen masters have taught as far back as the 1600s.[8] Indian gurus sometimes teach their students to relax sitting in a chair.

If you want to relax sitting cross-legged, there's a trick you need to know. It's easier if you sit on a firm cushion, and rest your feet off the edge of the cushion on the floor. The cushion helps to keep your back straight and reduces the strain on your back.

Pace yourself with your breath. When you scan each part of your body, do it for a few breaths instead of for a few seconds. Your breaths are the natural clock of your body, and when you pace yourself with your breath, you slow down to your body's natural rhythm. If you try to scan a part of your body for a few seconds instead of a few breaths, you'll end up feeling rushed and doing it for less time than you thought.

A typical relaxation session is about twenty to forty minutes long. Start slowly, with ten minutes a day and let your sessions grow naturally. If twenty to forty minutes a day sounds like a lot, think about how much time you spend feeling anxious or resentful every day.

It takes at least twenty minutes to begin to let go of your layers of tension. You can set a timer if you like, or just glance at a clock periodically. It's a matter of taste.

There is no upper limit to how long you can relax. The longer you relax, the more layers of tension you'll let go. At the end of some eight-week relaxation courses, students are guided through a four-hour relaxation session. Most of these people couldn't sit still eight weeks earlier, and now they're relaxing for four hours. At the end of the four hours most say that they feel like they're floating. The longer your relaxation session, the more relaxed you will be.

When is the best time to relax? It partly depends on your schedule and the people in your life. Most people prefer to relax in the morning when there are fewer distractions. I prefer the morning because later in the day there's always something that suddenly seems more important than relaxing. Another reason I like the morning is that it's the easiest time to relax. A relaxation session is the practice of letting go of tension, and like all practice, it's better to do it when it's easiest instead of when you need it the most.

Explain to everybody at home that you want to take a little time for yourself every day so that you can be more relaxed. If you've got a busy household, it can be hard to find a quiet time and place. But if your life is that busy, then you need to relax even more.

"There is only one path, but everybody must walk it in their own way."9

The Science and Medicine Behind Relaxation

Why does relaxing your body help to relax your mind? Tension comes from two parts in your brain. Mental tension comes from the upper part of your brain, also called the gray matter or cerebral cortex. It's where you dwell on the past or worry about the future.

Physical tension comes from your lower brain, also called the primitive brain or the brain stem. It's the part of your brain that's similar to a reptile brain and is responsible for the flight or fight response. The lower brain automatically tenses your muscles when you're under stress. I hesitate to call the cerebral cortex the higher brain because it's the part that usually causes most of the trouble.

Emotional tension gets translated into muscular tension. When you dwell on a past disappointment, the tension starts in your upper brain, but then your lower brain automatically converts your mental tension into physical tension. Your lower brain doesn't know why you're tense. It's the same as a reptile brain, which sees everything as a threat. Therefore your lower brain doesn't discriminate between different kinds of tension. It responds to all tension by getting your muscles ready to fight or run.

Whereas reptiles get tense for a reason, humans can get tense over nothing. Dwelling on a past embarrassment is enough to make us tense. So a silly little embarrassment that starts in your upper brain ends up making your entire body and mind tense.

Now here's the worst part. Because the two parts of your brain are interconnected, tension in one part of your brain feeds back and causes tension in the other part. Your lower brain feeds back and increases your anxiety, which makes you dwell on your tension even more. If you don't know how to break that cycle, it's easy to work yourself into a state of panic.

Why is it hard to relax by thinking you should relax? When you tell yourself to relax, you're using logic, which comes from your upper brain. But physical tension comes from your lower brain, and that part of your brain doesn't respond to logic. You can talk to yourself all you want and use all the logic you want, but your logic will stay in your upper brain. Your lower brain isn't wired to respond to logic. In other words, you can't tell yourself to relax because your reptilian brain doesn't respond to logic.

"It's hard to tell yourself to relax because the reptilian part of your brain doesn't respond to logic."

You *can* tell your lower brain to relax if you learn to speak speak its language. You have to tell your muscles to relax. If you relax your lower brain first, by relaxing your muscles, then your upper brain will follow. In other words, don't try to relax your mind. Focus on relaxing your body, and if you relax your body, your mind will follow.

Why is it hard to change when you're tense? If you understood the previous paragraphs, then you understand why it's hard to change when you're tense. When you're tense, your lower brain is in fight or flight mode.

The reptilian part of your brain thinks that every stress is a physical threat. It's wired to do what's familiar because that's the fastest response. There's no time to think when you're being chased by a predator. So even though you want to change, and you think that you'll be rational and try something new, when you're tense you'll still probably revert to what's familiar and wrong. Relaxation turns off the noise in your lower brain so that it doesn't get in the way of you making better decisions.

"When you are relaxed, you feel grounded, balanced, loose, and centered. During a relaxation session you practice producing those qualities so that you can reproduce them later."

5.
BREATHE FROM YOUR ABDOMEN

When you breathe as if you are relaxed, you become relaxed. The muscles in your chest are the second biggest store of tension in your body after the core muscles that control your posture. In this chapter you'll learn how to relax your chest muscles by breathing from your abdomen.

The Basics of Abdominal Breathing

Children naturally breathe from their abdomen, but most adults have forgotten how. If you still remember how to breathe from your abdomen, just skip to the next section.

To take in a breath, you push your abdomen out and breathe in at the same time. When you push your abdomen out, you draw down your diaphragm, which opens up your lungs and pulls air in.

To exhale, you let your abdomen relax, which pulls your abdomen back in, pushes up your diaphragm, and forces air out.

You'd think that breathing would be the most natural thing in the world, but when you're focused on the mechanics of how to breathe, suddenly it can seem complicated. An easy way to get started on an abdominal breath is by letting out a deep sigh. That pushes the air out of your lungs and relaxes your chest, which gets you ready to breathe in. By the way, don't worry that moving your abdomen in and out will distend your abdomen. If anything, it strengthens your muscles.

How to Relax Your Chest Muscles

The easiest way to relax your chest muscles is to feel your abdomen move as you breathe. Rest your hands on your navel (that's the area that moves the most when you breathe) and feel your abdomen move in and out. It's the same idea as feeling grounded, balanced, and loose. When you feel your abdomen move, you turn your focus inward and away from your tension. Feeling your abdomen move helps you become centered and in the moment. If you think about breathing but don't feel it, it's hard to be centered or in the moment.

Let your muscles relax between breaths. When you're grounded, balanced, and loose, you are in the moment, which makes it easy to relax between breaths. When you're tense, it's almost as if you're in a rush to get to the next breath, and your breaths become short and shallow. You'll know if you're letting your muscles relax between breaths if your whole abdomen moves in and out as you breathe. When you're tense, only the upper part of your abdomen will move with each breath. When you're relaxed, your entire abdomen will move with each breath.

Don't try to control your breaths. Some of your breaths will be deep, and some will be shallow. Just breathe from your abdomen, and let your breaths take care of themselves. If you try to control your breaths or try to make them all deep or even, you'll end up holding your breath instead of letting it flow.

Don't judge your relaxation. Sometimes it will be easy to relax, and other times it'll be hard. Don't put pressure on yourself to be perfect. When you judge your relaxation, you'll either become resentful that you're not relaxed or fearful that you can't relax. Either way, you'll build tension instead of letting it go.

There are a lot of things to focus on in the beginning, and it can be hard to keep track of them all and breathe naturally at the same time. It's normal to feel like you have to breathe consciously just to keep breathing in the beginning. But with a little practice you'll let your muscles relax, and your breaths will begin to flow. If you have a hard time juggling everything, just remember to focus on feeling your abdomen move in and out and the rest will come eventually.

"We are what we think.
All that we are arises with our thoughts.
With our thoughts we make the world. …
Speak or act with a pure mind
And happiness will follow you. …
Your worst enemy cannot harm you
As much as your thoughts, unguarded.
But once mastered,
No one can help you as much." [10]
– The Buddha

Variations of Breathing Techniques

There are many ways to breathe during mindbody relaxation. The most basic technique is abdominal breathing, which you just learned. Another variation is nostril breathing, where you focus on the sensation of your breath at the tip of your nose. In this case, you should feel the air move in and out past the tip of your nose, and it should feel like you're sniffing the air. A third breathing technique is called "ocean breathing," which is often used in yoga. In this case, you focus on the sensation of your breath at the back of your throat as you breathe in and out. It should feel like you're saying the words "Ahh-Haa" with each breath.

The constant in all of these variations is that you should feel your breath instead of think about it. When you feel your breath, you turn your thoughts into your body and away from your tension.

The advantage of abdominal breathing is that your abdomen is always moving as you breathe. If you focus on the air at the tip of your nose, there is a quiet phase at the end of each exhalation when there's little air movement to focus on.

Why Does Abdominal Breathing Help You Relax?

Breathing is the only body function that you can do in two completely different ways. You can either breathe from your chest, when you're active and need a lot of oxygen, or you can breathe from your abdomen, when you're resting and don't need a lot of oxygen. Each kind of breathing uses different muscles.

The muscles in your chest are *striated* muscles. They are the same kind of muscles that you also have in your arms and legs, which are good for producing maximum strength, but they don't relax easily. Your diaphragm is made of *smooth* muscles, which are the kind of muscles that you have in your blood vessels and intestines. They relax easily but don't build a lot of strength.

When you breathe from your chest, you're using striated muscles that are designed to produce maximum oxygen. The muscles between your ribs aren't big muscles, but there are a lot of them, and when you overuse them by breathing from your chest for a prolonged period of time, they build a lot of tension. Your diaphragm on the other hand is designed to relax easily between breaths. That's why abdominal breathing is the most relaxed and efficient way to breathe.

Breathing is a metaphor for your life. If you go through life trying to control things that you can't control, then both your life and your breathing will be tense. If you can let go of things that are beyond your control, both your breathing and your life will be relaxed.

"When you breathe as if you are relaxed, you will become relaxed."

6.
RELAX YOUR FACE

Your face is the tensest part of your body. You use your face to express your emotions and just as importantly to hide your emotions. Over time your face builds layers of tension, anxiety, and resentments that aren't always flattering.

To give you an idea of how much tension you have in your face, it helps to realize that you have almost as much of your brain devoted to controlling the muscles in your face as is devoted to controlling the muscles in the rest of your body. You have so much tension in your face that as you relax and become aware of your tension, your face will start to ache.

The easiest way to relax your face is with a gentle smile. A smile reaches up to your eyes and down into your jaw and soothes away the layers of tension. It doesn't have to be a big smile. In fact a big smile is easy to fake and doesn't help much. It's best if you're just aware of smiling. Being mindful of smiling gradually permeates the muscles of your face.

Smiling is so effective as a relaxation technique that it's sometimes used on its own. Just sit and gently smile for ten minutes and see how much more relaxed you feel. Smiling reminds you that the purpose of relaxation is to be happier. Relaxation shouldn't be solemn. If you forget to smile, or make your relaxation serious, you'll bring to your relaxation the very qualities you're trying to let go.

One of the things you notice about Buddhist monks is how easily they smile. They have a wonderful sense of humor and an easygoing nature about them because they aren't bound by tension. The simple act of smiling helps you let go of your layers of tension so that you can become the person you were meant to be.

"Wrinkles should merely indicate where smiles have been."[11]
– Mark Twain (1835–1910)

"Don't take life too seriously. You'll never get out alive."
– Bugs Bunny

How Relaxation Improves Your Appearance

On a more superficial note, smiling and relaxation can improve the way you look. Aging is not just the passage of time, but the accumulation of tension. The look of chronic tension takes a heavy toll that is unmistakable. Look around you. It's the face you see on most people most of the time: tight lips, clenched jaw, and hollow eyes. They look exhausted from the work of tension. Relaxation gives you an inner and outer beauty that cannot be faked. You will look, act, and feel noticeably younger. You will glow with inner peace.

"Aging is not just the passage of time, but the accumulation of tension."

7.
How to Stay Focused

To increase your focus during a relaxation session try repeating a word or phrase. Any sound, word, or phrase will do. You can say something as simple as "Let go of tension" silently to yourself. The technique works because when you repeat a phrase, it replaces the noise in your mind and helps you stay focused in the moment.

Repeating something also works by helping you recognize when you're not focused, because if you're not saying anything you're probably distracted and not focused on the moment.

Repeat a Word or Phrase

Here are a few suggestions of what you can say as you relax.

You can repeat your goals. "Let go of tension," "Scan your body," "Stop feeling rushed," "Be in the moment," "Breathe from your abdomen," "Let go of resentments," "Develop compassion," "Let go of fears," "Feel confident," "Gently smile," or "Feel centered."

You can say what you're feeling. If your mind is racing, you can remind yourself to "Be in the moment." If you are resentful, you can say, "Those are resentments; let them go." Naming what you're feeling helps you see it more clearly and makes it easier to let it go.

Another way to stay focused is to repeat a pleasant sound as you relax. Two-syllable sounds develop a nice rhythm when you repeat them: see-saw, let-go, in-ohm. You get the idea.

Breath counting is a traditional way to stay focused. You can say "in" as you breathe in, and count "one" as you breathe out, then "two," up to "five," at which point you start from "one" again. There are many ways to count your breath. Another alternative is to repeat the number several times as you exhale: "In. One, one, one. In. Two, two, two." It can help you stay focused if you're more distracted.

In Sanskrit the name for the word or phrase you repeat is *mantra*, which literally means instrument of thought. It's a simple idea that unfortunately carries a lot of mystical baggage, therefore I'll avoid using the term. The oldest known mantra is "Om."

Variations on the Basic Technique

There are two ways you can repeat a word or phrase. You can either say it independently of your breath, or you can synchronize what you say with your breath. If you repeat a word or phrase independently of your breath, the advantage is that you can speed up or slow down depending on how distracted you are.

How fast should you repeat a word or phrase? Say it as fast as you need to stay focused, but slow enough to be able to focus on feeling grounded, balanced, and loose.

If you chose to synchronize your words with your breath, the advantage is that you become more aware of your breathing, which helps you relax more completely between breaths. The disadvantage is that you can't speed up or slow down.

Match Your Words With the Stage of Your Relaxation

The words you repeat can reflect the stage of your relaxation. In the early stage of relaxation you might say, "Let go of tension." In the middle stage you might say, "That's a fear. Let it go." Later you might say, "Enjoy the moment and smile."

Sometimes I like to combine these methods and use different techniques depending on how distracted I am. I like to start off by repeating "Let go of tension" independently of my breath. I find that's the best way to quiet my racing mind. Then I switch to counting my breaths, because that helps me get even more relaxed and centered. When I've settled down after about ten minutes I begin to periodically name my tension and remind myself to let it go. Once I've settled down even more, I remind myself to enjoy the moment.

Even when I've relaxed, there are many times when my mind takes off again. When that happens I just go back to counting my breaths or repeating "Let go of tension." Sometimes I mix things up and say different words just to keep it fresh and to help me stay focused.

A parable about mantras puts all this in perspective. A simple farmer went to a wise teacher to learn how to meditate, and the teacher taught him how to meditate using Om. The farmer practiced every day, but made little progress. Finally, his teacher asked him what he did for a living, and the farmer said he grazed cows. "Very well," said the teacher. "Meditate on moo." Your mantra is only a tool.

Using Relaxation Tapes or CDs

There are tapes and CDs that can walk you through a relaxation session. Many people find them useful in the beginning. Ultimately you want to learn to relax without any props, so that your relaxation technique will be portable. You want to be able to relax anywhere and any time using just your body and breathing.

"Repeating a word or phrase helps you focus, replaces the noise in your mind, and helps you recognize when you're not focused."

8.

BECOME AWARE OF YOUR TENSION

Most people sleepwalk through life. They don't think about who they are or what they want to be, and then one day they wake up and wonder why they aren't happy. If you want to improve your life, if you want to be happier, you first have to understand how you've fallen asleep. In this chapter you'll learn how relaxation makes you aware of your tension and the obstacles to your happiness.

Recognize That You Are Tense

Recognizing that you are tense is harder than you might think. You've spent most of your life ignoring your tension or denying it. So in the beginning it won't be easy to see. If you have difficulty recognizing your tension, look for the indirect signs of tension, such as how easily you are distracted.

You'll be distracted when underlying tension rises to the surface and triggers a conscious thought. You'll be distracted when resentments or fears bubble to the surface and distract you. You'll be distracted so often that in the beginning you'll think you're doing something wrong or that you can't relax. But distractions are a normal part of relaxation. In fact it's normal to be distracted every few breaths. The trick to relaxation is to not get frustrated by your distractions and to use them to understand the underlying causes of your tension.

"You'll be distracted so often that in the beginning you'll think you're doing something wrong or that you can't relax."

The most common cause of distraction is not being in the moment. When you try to relax, you'll replay events from the past, or jump from thought to racing thought. You're so used to not being in the moment that your mind will do everything it can to be somewhere else.

You'll know if you're not in the moment if you're in a rush to relax. It sounds silly on paper, but here's how it can happen. As you try to relax, you'll think about all the other things you have to do and without even knowing it you'll be in a rush to relax. You won't think it exactly. You'll just start to go through the motions of your relaxation. When that happens, ask yourself what you're trying to accomplish. Do you want to do more things, or do you want to enjoy the things you do? Because you can't have it all.

Even recognizing that you're distracted can be difficult. You can have long trains of thought before you know it, and when you do recognize that you're distracted, you won't know how you got there or how long you've been gone. But with a little practice, you'll learn to quickly recognize your distractions, and with that you will begin to understand the underlying causes of your tension.

Dr. William James, one of the founders of modern psychology, was asked how long it was possible for a person to stay focused on a single object. After some reflection, he said that to the best of his knowledge, four seconds was the maximum.[12]

Everyone who has tried to relax has had to deal with distractions. The term "monkey mind" dates back to the Buddha, who compared the human mind to a restless monkey that "grabs one branch, and then letting go seizes another."[13]

Name the Underlying Cause of Your Tension

Psychotherapy is based on the idea that to deal with a negative emotion you first have to name it. In a relaxation session, you let go of your tension by first naming it. When you are resentful, say, "That's a resentment. Let it go." When you're worried, say, "That's a fear. Let it go." It's been medically proven that you use a different part of your brain and a different mental process to name your tension than you do to dwell on it.[14]

When you name your tension, you separate it from all the other things you're feeling, which makes it easier to let go. You shift from being controlled by your tension to controlling it.

Naming your tension helps you recognize it quickly next time. When you name your tension you file it away so that the next time you're tense you can recognize it quickly before it does any damage. During a relaxation session you practice recognizing your resentments and fears so that you can recognize them in the rest of your life.

In the beginning, you won't know what to call your tension. You'll just know that you feel unsettled or that your mind is racing. If you have a hard time naming your tension, try a few alternatives. For example, try saying, "Let go of fears," and you may see fears that you couldn't see before. Say, "Let go of resentments," and you may see resentments that you didn't know were there. The right words will ring true.

One specific cause of tension to watch out for is fear of criticism. You'll know if fear of criticism is a source of tension by how you criticize yourself when you try to relax. If you've been overly criticized in the past, you'll probably be a perfectionist and overly critical of yourself. You'll get frustrated if you don't relax right away, or you'll criticize your technique. It's as if the person who criticized you years ago is still looking over your shoulder. But now you're doing the work for them.

One technique that is sometimes helpful is to ask yourself what's preventing you from relaxing further. If you still don't know what to call your tension, don't try too hard. You'll see it when you're ready.

Don't Dwell on Your Tension

Naming your tension is not the same as dwelling on it. When you name your tension, name it as one of the four basic types: not being in the moment, resentments, fears, or trying to control things you can't control, and then let it go. Relaxation sounds like "That's a resentment. Let it go." It doesn't sound like "I'm resentful, and this is why."

Relaxation is also not the time to analyze your tension. When you're relaxed you'll be tempted to analyze what happened or why it happened. With the clarity of thought that comes from relaxation, it will seem like a good time to sort out your problems. But a relaxation session is the practice of letting go of tension, not the practice of dwelling on them. If analyzing your tension was such a good idea, you'd be relaxed by now.

Tension is not about what happened or why it happened, but the fact that you haven't let it go.

"Tension is not about what happened or why it happened, but the fact that you haven't let it go."

Naming Your Tension Shouldn't Be Uncomfortable

Looking at yourself isn't easy, but don't make it uncomfortable. You can decide how aware you want to be, and how deeply you want to look. It's not easy to admit that you're resentful or afraid.

It's hard to see your tension in the beginning and it's especially hard to see your layers of tension. You'll only see the superficial layers when you first start to relax. You may see that you're unsettled, but you won't know why. Later, as you relax, you may see that you're unsettled because you're in a rush, and you're in a rush because you've always been told to hurry up. Still later, you may see that you're in a rush because you're afraid that if you slow down you'll be criticized or called lazy.

Usually the top layers of tension are about not being in the moment. You'll be in too much of a rush to see the other layers. Once you allow yourself to relax and be in the moment, you will see if there are any deeper layers of tension. But as you do this remember to not dig for your tension. Look at what comes to the surface, name it, and let it go.

A classic parable about letting go involves two monks and a young woman. The two monks are out for a walk when they come across a young woman stranded by the side of a river. She can't get across the river because the bridge has been washed away. Without hesitating, one of the monks picks her up and carries her to the other side. The two monks then continue on their way. After some time the second monk turns to the first and says, "How could you have done that? How could you have picked her up and broken your vow of chastity? How could you have felt her soft skin against your face?" The first monk is a little surprised by his companion and says, "I let her go back there. Why do you still carry her?"

"When you're aware of your tension you can recognize it quickly before it does any damage."

9.
HOW MINDBODY RELAXATION WORKS

How does mindbody relaxation help you change your life and make you happier? So far you've learned how to relax during a relaxation session at home. In this chapter you'll learn how you can apply that technique to the rest of your day. Then in Part 3 of this book, you'll learn how you can use that technique to improve specific areas of your life. Here is a preview of how mindbody relaxation helps you improve your life.

- You practice becoming aware of your tension so that you can recognize when you're tense later.
- You practice letting go of your tension and living in the moment so that you can do that in the rest of your life.
- You practice feeling relaxed and in the moment so that you can recall that feeling later.
- You take time to escape from your tension so that you have more energy for the rest of your day.

You Become Aware of Your Tension

Tension is subtle and sometimes you don't know you're tense, you just know that everyone around you is annoying. During a relaxation session you practice recognizing your tension so that you can recognize it later. The faster you can recognize your tension, the faster you can let it go before it does any damage.

A relaxation session works by being a reflection of your life. How you do one thing is how you do everything. What makes you tense in life will also make you tense when you try to relax. If you dwell on the past during your daily life, you will be distracted by the past when you try to relax. If you dwell on your resentments, you will be distracted by your resentments. A relaxation session shows you how you spend your life.

> **"Tension is subtle and sometimes you don't know you're tense, you just know that everyone around you is annoying."**

Awareness is the first step of change. In order to be happy, you first have to understand how you make yourself unhappy. Once you're aware of how you make yourself unhappy, you can let it go and make room for change.

Unfortunately, awareness is a lesson you'll have to learn many times. One moment you'll know that you're wasting your life dwelling on the past and ten minutes later you'll turn around and do exactly the same thing. But at least when you're aware of your tension, you can catch yourself quickly before you waste more time on it. When you're not aware of your tension, you won't see that you're wasting your life until most of it is gone.

You Practice Letting Go of Tension

A relaxation session is the practice of letting go of tension and living in the moment. You practice letting go of your tension during a relaxation session so that you can let it go in the rest of your life. That's how it works.

A relaxation session makes you believe that you can change your life, because you see that you can relax and let go of things quickly during a relaxation session. Therefore you feel confident that you can do it in the rest of your life. You don't feel stuck with what you have. The ability to relax and be happy is not a gift that you're either born with or not born with – it's a skill that you can practice and improve.

What does letting go of tension mean? This is one of the most important lessons in relaxation. Letting go of your tension doesn't mean you'll never be tense again. Tension is unavoidable. Bad things will happen. You can't hope to permanently eliminate tension from your life. But you can learn to quickly let go of the tension that you feel, which is the next best thing. That is what turns the practice of relaxation into a coping skill.

> **"The ability to relax and be happy is not a gift that you're either born with or not born with – it's a skill that you can practice and improve."**

When you have a negative experience, when you deal with a difficult person, you can walk away from it and not let it spoil your day. You don't have to take it home with you. Ideally, you can let go of your tension almost immediately so that you won't waste any time on it.

A big part of letting go of tension means letting go of the past. It doesn't mean you'll never think about the past. You can't erase the past or pretend it didn't happen. But you can learn to quickly let go of the tension that you feel when you think about the past, which is the next best thing.

The combined effect of both of those skills, quickly letting go of your tension and letting go of the past, is enormous. If you can reduce your tension by even 20 percent, the effect on your life will be huge. During a relaxation session you practice being 100 percent relaxed and in the moment so that you can be at least 20 percent relaxed and in the moment later.

You will achieve the goals of relaxation by not focusing on them. It has been said that relaxation is goalless. But the truth is mindbody relaxation has two goals. The long-term goal is to be happier and healthier, and the short-term goal is to reduce your tension and live in the moment. Relaxation is goalless in the sense that you can achieve the long-term goals only by letting them go and focusing on the short-term goals.

The Indian monkey trap is a good example of doing the wrong thing under tension. The trap is made from a hollow section of bamboo that's just big enough for a monkey to slip its hand into. The trapper puts a piece of fruit inside the bamboo and then hides nearby. When he sees a monkey grab for the fruit, the trapper rushes the trap and panics the monkey. The elegance of the trap is that the monkey isn't caught by any spring-loaded mechanism or moving parts. The monkey traps itself. When the monkey grabs the fruit, it makes a fist that's too big to slip out of the bamboo, and when it's panicked, it can't think to let go of the fruit and save itself.

The lesson is clear. When you're tense, it's hard to see the big picture and to let go. Instead, you're more likely to react with what is familiar and often wrong. Free yourself by letting go of your tension.

You Practice Feeling Relaxed and In the Moment

It is not enough that you intellectually understand how to relax. You have to know how it feels to be to be relaxed so that you can access that feeling later. When you're caught up in the daily stress of life, sometimes you're not within reach of your right mind, and it's easy to forget that you even knew how to relax. A relaxation session helps you develop an emotional memory of how it feels to be relaxed and happy so that you can access that feeling later.

"A relaxation session helps you develop an emotional memory of how it feels to be relaxed and happy so that you can access that feeling later."

I can promise you that this will happen. After you've been relaxing for a few months, you'll think that you don't need to relax every day. You'll think that you can save a little time by practicing every other day. Everybody thinks that. I know I did. But once you stop practicing every day, you'll begin to lose your emotional memory of how it feels to be relaxed, and your tension will start to build again. Within a few days, little things will begin to irritate you again. You won't even notice it unless you're paying attention to it. If you continue to rely on knowing how to relax instead of the emotional memory of feeling relaxed, within a few more days you'll be back to your old self.

You don't learn how to relax. You practice being relaxed. Relaxation helps people lower their blood pressure. But if they don't practice every day, their blood pressure starts to climb again. When you're under stress every day, you have to work at being relaxed every day to stay relaxed.

"The trick is what one emphasizes. We either make ourselves miserable, or we make ourselves strong. The amount of work is the same."[15]
– Carlos Castaneda (1925–2000)

You Take Time to Escape Your Tension

A relaxation session is a mini-holiday. One of the reasons you enjoy holidays is because you get the chance to escape and enjoy the moment. Even a short break is reenergizing. But that feeling doesn't last very long after a holiday. By the end of the week you're back to your usual routine, and within two weeks you're as tense as ever.

The need to escape and relax is one of the essential coping skills of life. You need to be able to escape the stress of life in a healthy way, otherwise you'll get exhausted. If you become exhausted, you'll become irritable, and when you become irritable your tension will build and spill over into other areas of your life and hurt everything from your relationships to your health. (For more on how take care of yourself, see *Chapter 20: The Similarities Between Relaxation and Psychotherapy*.)

Relaxation is one of the few activities that you can use to escape and reward yourself and that is completely free and reliable. You can do it almost anywhere. It is an escape you can take every day.

Think of it this way. If something nice happens to you during the day, the rest of the day goes a little easier. Relaxation can be that thing. It can be a gift you give yourself every day.

Relaxation Gives You a Choice

You don't have to be relaxed all the time. Tension can be exciting. Sometimes you'll want to dwell on the past, worry about the future, relive your resentments, spin your wheels, or rush around and do many things at once. But there will also be times when you'll want to relax. And if you don't know how to relax, when those times come, you won't be able to relax.

The Essentials of Relaxation

What's essential to all relaxation techniques is what is constant over all of them. For example, some relaxation techniques teach you to sit with your left hand on top of your right, while others teach you to do the exact opposite. If how you placed your hands were essential to relaxation, there would be only one way of doing it. Since both techniques are used, how you place your hands can't be essential.

What is constant, and therefore what is essential, is that all relaxation techniques, either explicitly or implicitly, encourage you to do two things: relax your muscles and become aware of your tension. Here are the essentials in point form.

1. Don't try to relax your mind. Relax your muscles and your mind will follow.
2. There are three main areas of tension in your body: your core muscles, chest muscles, and face.
3. Become grounded, balanced, and loose, breathe from your abdomen, and be mindful of gently smiling. That is the most direct and efficient way to relax. There are other ways to relax. For example, you can relax by focusing on the light of a candle. But you still have to become grounded, balanced,

and loose. It's just that it happens unconsciously.

4. Become centered. Turn your focus into your body and away from your tension.
5. Name your tension so that you can recognize your tension later. When you're distracted, name the underlying cause of your tension, and let it go. Don't analyze your tension.
6. Relax for at least twenty to forty minutes a day. You need at least twenty to forty minutes to develop an emotional memory of how it feels to be relaxed and to gradually peel away your layers of tension.

The Difference Between Mindbody Relaxation and Meditation

There are many similarities between mindbody relaxation and meditation, but there is one important difference. Mindbody relaxation is based on the idea of letting go of tension. That is how it works. Meditation, on the other hand, is based on the idea of becoming mindful or aware of all your emotions and sensations and letting them go. I think that's what makes meditation seem mystical. It's not immediately clear why letting go of all your positive and negative emotions will improve your life.

The standard explanation of how meditation works is philosophical. But it's immediately clear how letting go of tension will improve your quality of life, because tension is the main obstacle to change and happiness.

People were more open to mysticism two and a half thousand years ago, but now we expect a more scientific explanation. Mindbody relaxation combines the best of traditional meditation with medicine and psychology to produce a self-help technique that is easily accessible.

Both mindbody relaxation and meditation are saying roughly the same thing, but they're saying it in a slightly different way. You will be happier when you reduce your tension. You will become enlightened when you see things as they really are, instead of through the distorted lens of tension. If you relax your body and become aware of your tension, you will transform your life.

"Mindbody relaxation is the practice of letting go of tension and being in the moment. You practice letting go of your tension, so you can let it go in the rest of your life."

10.
HOW IT FEELS

It's been said that trying to understand how relaxation feels by reading a book is like trying to understand the moon by looking at a finger pointing at the moon. The book only points you in the right direction. This chapter will try to describe some of the ways that mindbody relaxation does and does not feel.

Distractions

I've said this before, but it's so important I want to say it again. Distractions are a normal part of relaxation. The goal of mindbody relaxation is not to empty your mind or to eliminate distractions. An empty mind isn't good for anything. The goal of relaxation is to let go of your tension and enjoy your life. Therefore use your distractions to identify your tension and let it go.

Here's how the first ten minutes of my relaxation session feels. I start by trying to feel grounded, but within a few breaths I'm making up a list of things I have to do. I realize that I'm not in the moment and I tell myself, "Let it go. Be in the moment." I turn to focusing on my breathing. A few breaths later a truck drives by. I think, "Just when I was starting to relax." I mentally follow the truck as it drives away. It's making a lot of noise. I tell myself, "Let it go. Quit trying to control things that you can't control." I loosen my jaw. Out of nowhere a resentment pops into my head. I think of clever things that I could have said. I tell myself, "Let it go. Don't poison yourself." A few breaths later I'm back to dwelling on my resentment.

"The goal of mindbody relaxation is not to empty your mind. An empty mind isn't good for anything."

That's how it feels. And if I stopped relaxing before ten minutes were up I'd think that relaxation was impossible. But after about ten minutes the distractions become less intense. They're less in my face and easier to let go. After twenty years of practice I still get distracted just as often. The difference is that now I can quickly recognize when I'm tense and let it go.

The lesson you learn from relaxation is that you have little control over the thoughts that arise in your mind, and you cannot control the world around you. But you can let go of the tension that you feel, which makes all the difference.

The Chinese monk Hui-neng (637–713) was the first to emphasize the importance of letting go during relaxation. Before him, students were taught to empty their minds or purify their minds. Hui-neng said that a person with an empty mind is no better than "a block of wood or a lump of stone."[16] Our fundamental nature is already pure, he said.[17] Therefore our goal is to let go of the tension that is getting in our way.

Balance

Relaxation requires a balance between focusing too little and too much. The paradox is that if you try too hard to relax, you'll end up becoming more tense. The reason is that when you try too hard to relax, you're focused on the end result of becoming relaxed, instead of being in the moment where you can relax.

You'll know you're trying too hard if you're in a rush to relax, if you see your distractions as mistakes, if you forget to smile, or if you relax without joy. On the other hand, if you don't try hard enough to become grounded, balanced, loose, and centered, you won't be able to relax. You'll know you're not trying hard enough if you follow your distractions, daydream, or fall asleep.

> **"You'll know you're trying too hard to relax if you're in a rush to relax."**

Most of the time you'll be on one side or the other of that balance. But every once in a while you'll quit struggling and let yourself into the moment.

Focus

There are many things to focus on in mindbody relaxation because there are many places for your tension to hide. If you focus only on your breathing, your jaw could still be clenched. If you focus on your jaw, your toes could still be curled. In order to feel fully relaxed, you have to relax all of your body. One of the common mistakes people make is that they focus too much on relaxing one part of their body, usually their face, and then they unconsciously build tension somewhere else.

How much time should you spend on each part of your body? I usually spend about 50 percent of the time feeling grounded, balanced, and loose, 25 percent of the time focused on my breathing, and 25 percent of the time relaxing my face. But that varies greatly from day to day.

Spend several breaths on each part of your body before moving on to the next. Don't jump from spot to spot, because that probably means you're in a rush to relax, which means that you're not in the moment.

You'll know if you're too focused on one part of your body if you start to feel lighter. If you focus only on one part of your body, your core muscles will start to tighten up, and you'll become less grounded. You will feel lighter as your muscles tense up and lift you off the ground. You can fool yourself into thinking that feeling lighter is good. But you should always feel heavy and grounded when you're relaxed.

Some relaxation techniques encourage you to focus on only one thing – usually your breath. They are based on the same principle as mindbody relaxation. You turn your focus into your body and away from your tension. The main difference between those techniques is that they are less direct. For example, if you focus only on your breathing, you still have to become grounded, balanced, and loose, but it happens subconsciously.

The Rhythm of a Relaxation Session

Relaxation feels like long periods of distractions alternating with brief periods of calm. It's the opposite of what you might expect. Most people think that after a little practice they should be able to enter periods of uninterrupted bliss. But the first ten minutes of any relaxation session are full of distractions. That is the first wave of distractions.

After about ten minutes you'll begin to relax and then you'll have your first moment of pure calm. You'll be completely relaxed and in the moment, and it will feel like magic. But unfortunately it'll be gone in a flash. It will feel so wonderful that you'll want to stop and admire it, and the minute you do it will suddenly disappear. These moments of calm are so brief that it's been said they feel like "Here I am, wasn't I?"[18]

After the first moment of calm, you'll enter the next wave of distractions, and your mind will start to race again. This is a critical time. If you get discouraged because you couldn't hold on to the feeling of calm, you'll miss the point of relaxation. You can't eliminate distractions. Relaxation feels like two steps forward and one step back.

"A relaxation session feels like long periods of distractions alternating with brief periods of calm."

How you handle your distractions tells you a lot about how you handle tension in general. If you become discouraged by your distractions, you're probably a perfectionist and probably hard on yourself. Don't dwell on your distractions. If you focus on relaxing your body and don't try to relax your mind, you will start to calm down again after about five to ten minutes. Then you'll enter your second moment of pure calm, but this one will be deeper than the first.

Each moment of calm will be a little deeper than the one before. This is why long relaxation sessions are so relaxing, because they give you time to enter deeper states of relaxation. During a forty-minute session you'll probably have four or five moments of calm. They're so seductive that you'll be tempted to chase after them. But if you focus on being in the moment, you'll learn to flow with those magical moments instead of trying to control them.

Give yourself a one-hour relaxation session at least once a week. Once you've been practicing relaxation for about a month, give yourself a one-hour relaxation session at least once a week. You will experience a level of calm that's hard to describe. The longer your relaxation sessions are, the more relaxed you will feel.

Relaxation Is Not Quiet

There's a lot of talking to yourself during relaxation. You're either repeating a word or phrase, naming your tension, or reminding yourself to scan your body. And if you're not saying anything, you're probably not relaxing. But there's a difference between what you say during a relaxation session and the usual chatter that fills up your mind during the day. The things you say when you try to relax are about the moment, and repeating them helps to connect you with the moment.

Relaxation Is Not Sleepy

You normally have two states in life. You're either awake and anxious, or you're asleep and relaxed. Relaxation helps you discover a new way of being. You can be both awake and relaxed at the same time. Isn't that how you want to go through life? You want to be able to accomplish things but still be relaxed and efficient when you do them.

> **"Mindbody relaxation helps you discover a new way of being. You can be both awake and relaxed at the same time."**

The main reasons people feel drowsy during relaxation are that they've turned off their mind or they've tried to empty their mind. When you find yourself getting drowsy, focus more actively on feeling grounded, breathing more deeply, or saying your words more loudly to yourself. Some people try to avoid falling asleep by keeping their eyes open or slightly open, but most people find that a little too distracting. You can stay awake by being actively involved in your relaxation.

Relaxation Is Active

The common thread in the previous points is that relaxation is an active process. You don't just sit passively and hope to relax. That's what makes mindbody relaxation different from passive techniques like going for a walk or reading a book. When you go for a walk or read a book, you hope to relax. But sometimes you will relax and sometimes you won't. Mindbody relaxation is a technique that is reliable anywhere and any time if you do it actively.

Relaxation Is Simplicity

Relaxation is simple but deep. There is almost nothing new to learn, only something to let go. There is nothing new to find, you are already there. Just let go of the tension that's getting in your way and be free. Zen masters have tried to emphasize this simplicity by saying that relaxation should feel like "just sitting."

The difficult part of relaxation is keeping it simple. The more you practice, the more you'll be tempted to make it complicated. One common way that happens is that you'll forget to relax your body and instead try to relax your mind. It's your mind's way of trying to reassert itself and make things complicated.

**"In mindbody relaxation there is almost nothing
new to learn, only something to let go."**

You'll forget about the importance of relaxing your muscles and instead try to analyze the causes of your tension. You'll forget about naming your tension and instead get caught up in dwelling on your tension. You'll add layers of complication instead of taking them away. It's another way that relaxation is a reflection of your life. If you can make your relaxation simple, it will be easier to make your life simple.

"There are thousands upon thousands who have practiced meditation and obtained its fruits. Do not doubt its possibilities because of the simplicity of the method."[19]
– Zen Master Dogen (1200–1253)

Watching a Sunset

Relaxation is not something only gurus and monks can achieve. Everyone has had a relaxing moment. The most common relaxing experience is watching a sunset. There is a moment when you watch the sunset and you look out over the horizon and feel completely relaxed. That proves you can relax. You just need a little practice.

When you watch a sunset you don't feel sleepy or slow, instead you feel relaxed and alive. You may have had a disagreement earlier, but you can let it go. There may be noise in the background, but it doesn't bother you. A relaxation session should feel as peaceful and uncomplicated as watching a sunset.

The Medical Evidence

Neuroscientists at Harvard University have shown that people who do mindbody relaxation regularly are happier than people who don't. It's known that the frontal part of the brain regulates emotions, and the left frontal region is associated with positive emotions. The Harvard neuroscientists scanned the brains of people who meditate regularly and showed that the left frontal part of their brains were more active while they were meditating.[20] That says that meditation feels good, which is interesting in itself.

> **"Neuroscientists have shown that people who relax regularly are happier than people who don't."**

A subsequent study showed something even more interesting. People who meditate regularly not only had more activity in the positive region of their brains while they were meditating, they also had more activity in that region when they weren't meditating. They weren't just happier while they were meditating, they were happier in general.

Dr. R. Davidson of the University of Wisconsin took this study one step further. He scanned the brains of Tibetan monks who had been meditating for years. The activity in their left frontal region was off the charts. It was much higher than non-meditators and significantly higher than "casual" meditators.[21]

The Qualities of Relaxation

When people try to describe how mindbody relaxation feels, they often use similar words to describe their individual experiences. Here are the most common descriptions.

Relaxation feels clear. You clear your mind of tension, and it is that clarity that allows you to experience the other qualities of relaxation. Tension clouds your mind and prevents you from feeling anything other than anxiety and dissatisfaction.

Relaxation feels joyful. There is a unique joy that comes from being relaxed and in the moment. It's the joy of being comfortable in your own skin. It's the peace and happiness you've been looking for.

Relaxation feels compassionate. You let go of the fears and resentments that are getting in your way, and you can embrace the world around you.

Relaxation feels free. You feel like a weight has been taken off your shoulders. You feel buoyant and alive.

Relaxation feels energizing. Tension is exhausting. Hanging on to all those resentments and fears is hard work. Relaxation revitalizes you.

Relaxation feels magical. One of the defining qualities of a transcendent experience is that it is impossible to describe to someone else. Therefore there is no point in trying further. You will know how relaxation feels once you've experienced it, and when you have, you will know it has the power to transform your life.

> **"Mindbody relaxation is not passive, empty, quiet, or sleepy. It is as simple as just sitting, as enjoyable as watching a sunset, and as revitalizing as an escape."**

11.
HELPFUL GUIDEPOSTS

Here are some of the common obstacles to relaxation and answers to some of the frequently asked questions about relaxation.

The Two Most Common Obstacles to Relaxation

The more tense you are, the more you'll think that you don't need to relax. Despite knowing the consequences of being tense, when you're tense, you'll think that you don't need to relax. The more tense you are, the more you'll think that a little tension is good for you or that it defines who you are. You'll try to convince yourself that something as simple as relaxation can't possibly help you.

Driven personalities are initially more reluctant to let go of their tension. They think that it has given them an edge or that they'll slow down without it. But tension doesn't make you think faster. It only makes you think you're thinking faster. The reason the Samurai warriors were so effective was that they practiced being in the moment. Not bound by tension, they were fast and flexible.

A clear mind is not empty – it is open. A quiet mind is not passive – it is efficient. If you're reluctant to let go of your tension, you have misunderstood the goal of relaxation. Relaxation doesn't make you passive. Letting go of things you can't control isn't a sign of weakness. It's efficient. Relaxation doesn't mean letting go of what's important. It means letting go of what's holding you back.

> **"A clear mind is not empty – it is open. A quiet mind is not passive – it is efficient."**

Don't be in a rush to relax. The second most common obstacle to relaxation is being in a rush to relax. You'll think about all the other things you have to do, and without you even knowing it, you'll be in a rush to relax. You'll go through the motions of your relaxation instead of actively relaxing. When you're in a rush to relax, ask yourself what you're trying to achieve. Do you want to do more things, or do you want to enjoy the things you do? It's a simple point, but important to remember.

"Life is short and no one knows what the next moment will bring. Open your mind while you have the opportunity."[22]
– Zen Master Dogen (1200–1253)

Problems and Frequently Asked Questions

It is normal to feel more anxious in the beginning. There are so many things to focus on in the beginning that it's natural to feel more tense when you're learning to relax. If you're a perfectionist, you'll probably feel even more tense. You'll judge your-self and feel disappointed when you're distracted. That initial anxiety usually wears off after a few weeks. But if it persists, try reducing your relaxation time to five or ten minutes a day and then let it grow naturally.

Don't worry about itches and aches. When you start to re-lax, you'll immediately be confronted with the problem of what to do with your itches and aches. If you try to ignore them, you may end up making yourself more tense. Most people au-tomatically assume that they have to sit perfectly still during relaxation. A little moving around won't disturb anything. The trick to dealing with these minor distractions is to remember to breathe through them, because you build tension when you hold your breath.

You will deal with the same issues repeatedly. The same people and the same memories will keep distracting you and making you tense. You've spent a lifetime building many of those resentments. Don't expect to let them go after just a few months of relaxation. But each time you let go of another lay-er of tension, your resentments will become less emotionally charged.

Don't expect your progress to be smooth. Once you've been relaxing for a few months, you will probably enter a phase when it will get harder to relax. Usually it will happen because you've stopped being active in your relaxation or because you've stopped focusing on the basics. Remember – don't focus on re-laxing your mind, instead focus on relaxing your body.

You may need to relax even more during stressful times. Twenty to forty minutes a day is just a guideline. If you're go-ing through a stressful time, you may want to add a second re-laxation session to your day. The problem is that when you're tense, you'll think that you're too busy to relax. You'll think that you just need to work harder and dig yourself out of this hole, and then you can go back to relaxing later. I understand that you may not always have the time to relax for a long time. But if you trade relaxation for work too often, after a while it will become easy to pass on relaxation. And I don't think it should ever be easy.

Don't spend more energy than you conserve. Relaxation conserves your energy because you're not wasting energy feeling tense. Busy people sometimes take that newfound energy and do even more with it. They work longer hours, or sleep less, and do all the things that made them tense in the first place. See your new energy as a gift and save it for what's important.

"The best is the enemy of the good."[23] Even with the best of intentions, you won't always have twenty to forty minutes to relax every day. When you're pressed for time, you'll be tempted to skip your relaxation and save it for when you can "do it right." If you don't have twenty minutes, try relaxing for ten minutes a day. Ten minutes a day is still better than relaxing for sixty minutes just once a week.

Don't end your relaxation session abruptly. Take a few breaths at the end of your relaxation session to stretch and gradually get back into the day. If you jump up quickly and rush off, it probably means you were never in the moment.

12.
A One-Month Relaxation Program

This is a one-month relaxation program to introduce you to the basics of relaxation. By the end of the month you should feel more relaxed and happy.

Week One

Start by relaxing for ten minutes a day in the morning. Lie down and rest your hands on your abdomen. Begin by feeling grounded, balanced, and loose. Mentally scan each point where your back touches the ground, and feel the contact you make. Scan each area for several breaths. Don't rush through it. Every time you get distracted, remember – don't try to relax your mind, instead focus on relaxing your body.

After several breaths, shift to relaxing the muscles in your chest. Feel your abdomen move in and out as you breathe and let your muscles relax between breaths. After several more breaths, try to relax your face muscles by gently smiling.

Finally, begin to repeat something to yourself. Say, "Let go of tension. Let go of tension," independently of your breath. Say it as fast as you need to eliminate the chatter in your mind, but slow enough to focus on everything else. Spend the rest of the ten minutes focused on those four things: your body, breathing, face, and words.

Week Two

In the second week, increase your relaxation time to twenty minutes a day. Focus on the same four things you did before, but this week introduce awareness into your relaxation. Every time you get distracted, name the underlying cause of tension, then let it go by relaxing your body. Keep it simple. Name your tension as one of the four basic types: not being in the moment, resentments, fears, or trying to control things you can't control. If you have difficulty naming your tension, just say, "Let go of tension."

With a longer relaxation session, you may begin to experience moments of pure calm. In a twenty-minute session, you'll probably have one or two of moments of pure calm. Don't chase after them. Just let them flow by being in the moment.

"The greatest discovery of my generation is that human beings can change the quality of their lives by changing the attitudes of their minds."[24]
– William James (1842–1910)

Week Three

In the third week, increase your relaxation sessions to half an hour. You won't add anything new during the third week. You will just practice on improving and enjoying your technique.

There is a milestone that most people reach during the first month. They're able to let go of their tension despite being distracted, and they begin to use their distractions to learn more about themselves. Sometime in the first three to four weeks, you'll probably reach that milestone.

At the end of the third week, give yourself a one-hour relaxation session on the weekend and see how much more relaxed you feel.

Week Four

In the fourth week, increase your practice to forty minutes a day. Break it up into two twenty-minute sessions if you have to. In this week you'll practice applying your technique to your daily life.

When you're tense during the day, name your tension. Then let go of your tension by relaxing your body and becoming grounded. Take a few breaths to scan the soles of your feet. Feel the soles of your feet, instead of trying to visualize them. Your body will be ready to run or fight when you're tense, and you won't be grounded. Become grounded by feeling the contact you make with the ground and with your chair. Relax your chest, and then return to your work. Don't let your tension build. Catch it quickly before it becomes another layer of resentments or fears.

If you practice mindbody relaxation every day for a month, you will feel more relaxed and happy. If you practice every day for a year, it will transform your life.

Test it for yourself. Don't take my word for it that relaxation is good for you. Try the following test and see for yourself. Relax every day for a month, then stop for a few days and notice the difference. If relaxation was effective, you'll notice your tension start to rise and your tolerance start to evaporate.

You'll feel less comfortable and more anxious during the day. Then, complete the experiment by going back to relaxing every day and seeing how quickly those symptoms disappear. It never ceases to amaze me how much more relaxed I feel when I relax every day.

"If you relax every day for a month, you will feel more relaxed and happy. If you relax every day for a year, it will transform your life."

SUMMARY

There are four basic causes of tension: not being in the moment, resentments, fears, and trying to control things you can't control.

When you're tense, you tend to do what's familiar and wrong instead of what's new and right.

The key to relaxation is – don't try to relax your mind. Focus on relaxing your body.

There are three main areas of tension in your body: your core muscles, chest muscles, and face.

Relax your core muscles by becoming grounded, balanced, and loose. Scan the points where your body touches the ground, and notice how each point feels. Don't try to visualize where you touch the ground – feel it.

Become balanced. Imagine the four corners of your feet or the four corners of your seat and distribute your weight evenly.

Relax your chest muscles by feeling your abdomen move in and out as you breathe. Let your muscles relax between breaths.

Be aware of gently smiling and relax the muscles in your face.

Become centered. Turn your thoughts into your body and away from your tension.

Your body exists in the moment, and when you focus on your body you connect with the moment.

Repeat a word or phrase to help you stay focused and to recognize when you're not focused.

When you're distracted, name the underlying cause of tension. Don't try to analyze your tension. Just name it and let it go.

When you're aware of your tension you can catch yourself quickly the next time you become tense.

Relax for twenty to forty minutes a day. Try to relax for an hour once a week.

PART 3.
12 WAYS TO IMPROVE YOUR LIFE

13.
BEGIN BY IMPROVING YOUR SELF-ESTEEM

Before you change anything in your life, have a look at yourself. If you don't like who you are, you probably won't be happy with the rest of your life, no matter how good it might be. In other words, the pursuit of happiness begins with your self-esteem. In this chapter you'll learn

- How tension damages your self-esteem.
- The symptoms of poor self-esteem.
- How letting go of tension improves your self-esteem.

The Definition of Self-Esteem

Self-esteem is a combination of two traits: self-efficacy and self-respect.[25]

- Self-efficacy is the confidence that you can face life's challenges, and that you have something worthwhile to offer.

- Self-respect is the confidence that you deserve to feel happy, and that other people don't have to fail in order for you to be happy.

Self-efficacy is intellectual confidence, and self-respect is emotional confidence. Professionally successful people have self-efficacy but sometimes lack self-respect.

How Tension Causes Poor Self-Esteem

The most common cause of poor self-esteem is destructive criticism. You know what destructive criticism sounds like. "Don't be silly." "You'll never amount to anything." "You think you're funny, don't you?" "I hate it when you do that." "Don't be stupid."

Small doses of destructive criticism are normal. Everyone has heard it before. But the goal of constructive criticism is to inspire change, and the effect of destructive criticism is the exact opposite. It's shaming and dismissive. It usually functions as an outlet for the other person's tension instead of as a motivation for change. Although small doses of destructive criticism are normal, if you've been exposed to enough of it you begin to believe it, and after a while it can damage your self-esteem.

Every person responds to destructive criticism differently. How you respond to it depends on a combination of how sensitive you are to criticism and how strong your coping skills are. Some people have been exposed to a lot of destructive criticism and still have a healthy self-esteem, while others have been exposed to little destructive criticism and still end up suffering with poor self-esteem.

"The underlying emotion of poor self-esteem is fear."

The underlying emotion of poor self-esteem is fear. The more you've been criticized, the more you're afraid of being criticized. You're afraid of what other people think about you. You wonder if they like you, or if you've done something that will make them think less of you. The effect of destructive criticism is that you're afraid of doing or saying anything wrong because the smallest mistake could expose you to more criticism or ridicule.

So how do you improve your self-esteem? You don't improve your self-esteem by working harder or trying to be more perfect. That never fills the void of poor self-esteem. You improve your self-esteem by letting go of the fears that undermine your self-esteem.

The Self-Esteem Test: 4 Questions

The impact of destructive criticism is so profound and its consequences are so predictable that if you've been exposed to enough destructive criticism, you will almost certainly have some of the following traits.

1. Do you feel ashamed of who you are or what you feel inside? If you've been exposed to destructive criticism, you feel uncomfortable in your own skin. You feel that if people knew the real you, nobody would like you. You think that other people are happier than you or that they have something you're missing. You feel "less than" because that's the message you receive from destructive criticism.

2. Do you always feel in a rush? The most common criticism children hear is "hurry up." Children don't live on the same timetable as adults. They're happy to live in the moment. So they're always being told to hurry up. You've probably been told to hurry up so many times that there's a voice inside you always telling you to hurry up. When someone tells you to hurry up, the underlying message is this: don't live in the moment, always be in a rush, and most of all don't take time for yourself. They are also indirectly saying that your time doesn't count. The result is that when you grow up, you probably find it hard to take time for yourself. You're afraid that if you do you'll be called selfish or lazy.

3. Do you feel as if there's someone looking over your shoulder, ready to criticize you most of the time? "You could have done better. You're lazy. Don't be stupid." Whose voice do you hear saying that? If you've been criticized excessively growing up, you expect to be criticized. The effect of destructive criticism is that you don't wait to hear what other people are telling you. You go directly to what you think they're saying and you react defensively. People with poor self-esteem are often seen as arrogant when they're actually being defensive.

4. Do you have difficulty admitting your mistakes? Do you become aggressive, sarcastic, or withdrawn when you're corrected? If you've been exposed to excessive destructive criticism, the thought of hearing more criticism is too much to bear. When someone tries to give you helpful advice, all you hear is that voice of destructive criticism that you heard years ago. Some people respond to that fear by being quick to criticize others. You may be the first to notice the slightest mistake in other people. If destructive criticism is all you've known, destructive criticism of others is the easiest pattern to fall into.

Even successful people can suffer from poor self-esteem. In their case, the details are slightly different but the symptoms are the same. Professionally successful people aren't paralyzed by fear because they're driven by talent or rebellion. But their self-image remains distorted. Therefore they can't enjoy their success, no matter how much they achieve. Nothing ever feels enough for them. So they continue to work long after someone else would have stopped, hoping to fill that void.

How To Improve Your Self-Esteem

You improve your self-esteem by identifying the fears that undermine your self-esteem, letting them go, and learning something better in their place. You improve your self-esteem by applying the principles of self-change that you practice in mindbody relaxation. During a relaxation session, you will see if fears play a role in your self-esteem by how often fears distract you. Do you feel rushed? Do you dwell on past criticisms? Do you feel there's someone looking over your shoulder?

> **"You improve your self-esteem by identifying your fears, letting them go, and learning something better in their place."**

Once you identify your fears, you then have to let go of your fears to create room for a healthier self-image. During a relaxation session you practice letting go of your fears so that you can let them go when you confront them in your daily life. When you're distracted by a fear, name it and let it go. Later, when someone makes a critical remark, you don't have to dwell on it and turn it into more than it is. You can let it go quickly because you practiced letting it go earlier. You can focus on more important things, which increases your chances of success, which further increases your self-esteem.

Mindbody relaxation not only helps you identify your fears and let them go, it also helps you replace them with a healthier self-image. You learn how to live in the moment, instead of living in the past. You learn how to practice self-care, instead of not taking time for yourself. The act of relaxation is self-care. You're saying that you're worth taking time for, which is the basis of self-respect. It won't happen overnight. But just as repeated negative messages can distort your self-esteem, repeating positive messages can repair it.

Consider the case of Andrew, a successful entrepreneur who owned his own computer company. By any measure Andrew was successful. But he grew up in a cold and critical environment that had an effect on him later on. Both his parents were professors, and although they rarely scolded him, their way of motivating him was to ignore him if he didn't live up to their expectations. This was destructive criticism through omission.

Andrew was obviously gifted, but he doubted himself. After each success he would be exuberant for a few days, but then would doubt himself again. Over the years his drinking became heavier and heavier as a way of coping with his emotional pain. He wondered if people could see past his facade. He wondered why his wife was still with him. He wondered if she was having an affair. His wife was supportive and came to all his appointments, but I could tell she was losing patience.

I encouraged Andrew to practice relaxation and to name the fears that came up during his relaxation. Because Andrew was so intelligent, I emphasized that he shouldn't try to analyze his fears or to follow them. Once he named his fears, the goal was to quickly let them go and return to relaxing his body. Within six months, even his wife noticed that Andrew was more comfortable in his own skin, and their relationship began to improve.

How to Prevent Poor Self-Esteem

Poor self-esteem is preventable. Criticism is a necessary part of life. Everybody makes mistakes and everybody needs to be corrected. But criticism doesn't have to lead to poor self-esteem. Children can grow up to be happy and productive if they're taught two kinds of lessons. The first kind of lesson is the traditional lesson, or what they need to learn. The second kind of lesson is how to let go of the tension produced by the first lesson. Without the second lesson, corrections that are meant to help them will eventually get in their way. Corrections that are done with the best of intentions can still lead to poor self-esteem. I think teaching relaxation techniques should be part of every curriculum.

The importance of both criticism and relaxation is emphasized in the complementary philosophies of China – Confucianism and Taoism.

"Confucianism…preoccupies itself with conventional knowledge, and under its auspices children are brought up so that their originally wayward and whimsical natures are made to fit the Procrustean bed of the social order…. Confucianism presides, then, over the socially necessary task of forcing the original spontaneity of life into the rigid rules of convention. The function of Taoism is to undo the inevitable damage of this discipline."[26]
– Alan W. Watts (1915–1973)

"You don't improve your self-esteem by working harder or trying to be more perfect. You improve it by letting go of the fears that undermine your self-esteem."

14.
IMPROVE YOUR HEALTH

Tension damages every organ and system in your body. It directly or indirectly contributes to most diseases. In this chapter you'll learn how tension causes disease, and how relaxation prevents and treats a number of diseases.

How Tension Causes Illness

Tension causes premature aging of DNA. The link between tension and disease was first proven in a study at the University of California at San Francisco. The study showed that mothers who have chronically ill children and are under high stress have more damage to their DNA than mothers with healthy children.[27]

The study looked at thirty-nine mothers who had chronically ill children and compared them to a similar group of mothers with healthy children. Both groups were matched in every other way (age, weight, etc.). The study showed that the mothers with chronically ill children had DNA that was prematurely older than the mothers with healthy children. In other words, tension causes aging at the cellular level.

How did the researchers know that the DNA was prematurely older? If you're interested in the biology behind the answer, continue reading this paragraph. If not, just skip to the next paragraph. The lifespan of a cell is determined by a special strand of DNA called a "telomere" that caps the end of each chromosome. Each time a cell divides, part of the telomere is used up, which makes a telomere act like molecular countdown clock. When a telomere gets below a certain length, the chromosome becomes unstable, and the cell dies. The study showed that the mothers with chronically ill children had significantly shorter telomeres, which means significantly older DNA, than the mothers with healthy children.

"Tension causes premature aging at the cellular level, which leads to a variety of diseases."

The implications of this discovery are huge. Premature aging at the cellular level leads to a varity of diseases. If the cells that line your blood vessels prematurely age due to tension, you may end up with heart disease. If the cells of your immune system prematurely age, you will be more susceptible to everything from pneumonia to cancer. If the collagen cells that support your face prematurely age, your skin will lose its elasticity and wrinkle. In other words, this one study explains the many diverse consequences of tension.

Can reducing tension reduce disease? The answer is yes. Numerous studies have shown that relaxation can help treat high blood pressure, migraines, fibromyalgia, irritable bowel syndrome, psoriasis, asthma, and cardiac arrhythmias, to name a few.[28] Mindbody relaxation helps your body help itself, which is the most powerful form of medicine.

Norman Cousins was the editor of *Saturday Review* for almost four decades. In his fifties he developed a serious medical disease that he treated with a combination of laughter therapy, in consultation with his sometimes skeptical physicians. One time, while in hospital, he told his doctors, "Gentlemen, I want you to know that you're looking at the darnedest healing machine that's ever been wheeled into this hospital." He went on to write a number of books about the power of the body to cure itself and became adjunct professor of medicine at UCLA. He wrote, "Proper health education should begin with an awareness of the magnificent resources built into the human system."[29]

Below are some of the studies that have proven that relaxation prevents and treats disease.

Reduce the Risk of Heart Disease

Heart disease is the number one cause of death in the developed world. One study in the *British Medical Journal* looked at a group of 192 men and women.[30] The participants were randomly divided into two groups. Both groups were given information on lowering blood pressure, reducing animal fats, and stopping smoking. One group was also given an eight-week course on relaxation.

After only eight weeks, the relaxation group had significantly lower blood pressure. After eight months the relaxation group continued to have lower blood pressure. Four years later, not only did the relaxation group have lower blood pressure, they also had a significantly lower rate of heart disease and fewer fatal heart attacks. The simple technique of mindbody relaxation significantly reduced the risk of the number one cause of death in the developed world. The personal, social, and economic consequences of this are enormous.

"Mindbody relaxation can reduce the risk of heart disease, the number one cause of death in the developed world."

Reverse Hardening of the Arteries

Another study showed that relaxation can reverse arteriosclerosis. The results were published in the American Heart Association journal, *Stroke*.[31] The study looked at sixty patients and measured the hardening and clogging of their arteries using ultrasound.

The patients were randomly divided into two groups. One group received health education, while the other group was also taught how to relax. Nine months after the initial ultrasound readings were taken, the hardening and clogging of their arteries was measured again. Amazingly, the relaxation group had actually reduced the hardening and clogging of their arteries. They had less arteriosclerosis than the non-relaxation group.

How can mindbody relaxation reverse hardening of the arteries? It can happen on many levels. Relaxation reduces stress hormones like adrenaline and cortisol that are known to contribute to arteriosclerosis. Relaxation also reduces blood pressure that is known to cause hardening of the arteries. To understand how this might happen, you have to realize that you can temporarily increase your blood pressure by holding your breath.

Definitely don't try this, but if you hold your breath and tighten your chest muscles as if you're having a temper tantrum, your blood pressure will rise temporarily. The effect happens because when you hold your breath, you increase the pressure in your chest, which makes your heart pump harder to keep your blood moving, which increases your blood pressure.

Now imagine if you did that a little bit with every breath. Each time you don't let your chest muscles relax between breaths, you're constantly making your heart work harder. Over time that little difference can have a large cumulative effect on your blood pressure, causing hardening of your arteries.

Incredibly, this study showed that the reverse is also true. If you breathe from your abdomen and let your chest muscles relax between breaths, you will lower your blood pressure and reverse hardening of the arteries.

Strengthen Your Immune System

One study took forty-one volunteers and randomly divided them into two groups.[32] The strength of their immune system was measured by the strength of their antibody response to the flu vaccine. One group was given an eight-week relaxation course, while the control group was not. At the end of the eight weeks, both groups were given an influenza vaccine. The results showed that the relaxation group had a significantly greater antibody response, and therefore had a stronger immune system, than the non-relaxation group. That in itself is noteworthy.

But the study also had a second part. Previous studies had shown that people who meditate regularly have more activity in the area of the brain associated with positive emotions. This study confirmed those results and also showed that individuals with the highest positive brain activity had the strongest immune systems.

Increase Life Expectancy

Relaxation not only reduces the risk of heart disease, it also increases life expectancy according to a study published in the *American Journal of Cardiology*.[33] The study randomly divided 202 patients into two groups. Both groups received standard health education and high blood pressure treatment, while one group was also taught how to relax. Both groups were followed for eight years.

During those eight years, the relaxation group had 30 percent fewer deaths from cardiovascular disease and 23 percent fewer deaths from all causes. To put this in perspective, a medical treatment is considered successful if it can reduce heart disease by 10 percent. To reduce heart disease by 30 percent is remarkable. To reduce overall deaths by almost a quarter is amazing.

"Relaxation can reduce the risk of death due to heart disease by 30 percent."

Improve Your Sleep

Poor sleep is one of the common complaints that people have when they're tense. They either have difficulty falling asleep, or they have poor quality of sleep. Sleep is related to many aspects of health. It has even been shown that people who sleep less than seven to eight hours a night are more likely to be overweight.[34] Relaxation can improve your sleep. But before you turn to relaxation to improve your sleep, take a look at the other obvious obstacles to sleep, such as too much caffeine or excessive alcohol.

There is a specific technique that you can use to improve your sleep. Lie in bed, relax your body and become grounded, balanced, loose, and centered as you learned in part 2 of this book. But instead of being active during relaxation, allow yourself to be more passive. Don't name the underlying causes of your tension. When you're distracted, let go of your tension and return to relaxing your body.

Turn off your mind and imagine that you're looking at a black screen and that your surroundings are completely black. Slowly go through each part of your body, letting go of tension and relaxing your muscles. Gradually your mind will relax and you will drift off to asleep. Your sleep will be deep and restful because you will have relaxed both your body and mind.

The Short Medical History of Relaxation

The medical history of relaxation is surprisingly brief. One of the first doctors to consider the importance of relaxation was Dr. Edmund Jacobson of the University of Chicago. In the 1920s he developed a technique called "progressive relaxation," in which he taught patients to progressively relax their muscles.[34] The technique is still used today.

The medical history of relaxation is so brief that before 1960 most languages didn't even have a word for stress. The pioneering work on the physiology of stress was done by Dr. Hans Selye of the University of Montreal, who showed the physical consequences of stress on the immune system.[35] When asked to present a series of papers in Europe, Dr. Selye had to coin the words *le stress* and *der stress*. He also coined the word *stressor*, which has become part of our vocabulary.

Shortly after Dr. Selye's work was published, Dr. Herbert Benson, a cardiologist at Harvard, began to study the medical benefits of relaxation. Dr. Benson made two fundamental contributions to the study of relaxation.

First, he showed that relaxation had a real physiological effect that could be measured. It wasn't just an illusion. People could lower their blood pressure, slow their heart rate, and calm their brain waves. He called that effect "the relaxation response." That was important because once relaxation could be measured, it could be studied scientifically.

His second contribution was to remove the mysticism surrounding relaxation. He showed that if people followed a few basic rules they could quickly learn to relax and receive the benefits of relaxation.

In 1975 Dr. Benson wrote a popular book called *The Relaxation Response*.[36] In the preface to the 2000 edition, he wrote, "Western science had not, in the nineteen sixties, begun to entertain the possibility that physical problems might be rooted in mental or emotional activity, or that stress as a phenomenon could engender demonstrable physical problems."[37]

It's hard to believe that just a few years ago doctors didn't think there was a significant connection between the body and mind. They didn't think that your emotional state could cause physical problems, or that physical problems could hurt your emotional state. The few doctors who dared challenge that dogma did so at considerable risk to their professional careers and were subject to the scorn of their colleagues. Medicine has come so far in such a short period of time that it is hard to imagine how confidently ignorant it once was.

I believe that mindbody relaxation will play an even bigger role in the future of medicine. Medicine is not just about treating people – it is about healing them. And healing involves helping the body and mind discover their inner strength after an illness. Healing involves treating the body, mind, and soul as one.

"The witch doctor succeeds for the same reason all the rest of us [doctors] succeed. Each patient carries his own doctor inside him. They come to us not knowing that truth. We are best when we give the doctor who resides within each patient a chance to go to work."[38]
– Albert Schweitzer (1875–1965)

**"Mindbody relaxation helps your body help itself,
which is the most powerful form of medicine."**

15.
LOSE WEIGHT

Losing weight and keeping it off is one of the hardest things to do. Weight loss is not just a matter of eating less or eating healthier foods. If it was that simple, most people would have done it by now. But one-third of Americans are obese. In this chapter you'll learn how tension leads to overeating and how relaxation increases the chances of success of all weight loss programs.

People overeat for the same reasons that other people use drugs or alcohol. They overeat to escape, relax, or reward themselves. Overeating isn't about hunger. It's emotional eating. It has been shown that overeating acts on the same part of the brain as drug addiction.[39]

To see the connection between tension and overeating, consider the times when you're more likely to overeat. You usually overeat when you feel

- Angry or frustrated
- Lonely or isolated
- Tired

How do you feel at the end of the day? You're probably angry if you've had a tough day at work or a tough commute home. Perhaps you have a job where you have to respond to other people's needs all day. You may feel lonely if you're isolated. You don't have to be physically alone to feel lonely. And you're probably tired. That's why the strongest cravings for emotional eating usually occur at the end of the day.

At the end of the day you're so tense that you forget the promises you made to yourself earlier in the day about healthy eating. You just want to relax and comfort yourself. In other words, when you're tense you tend to do what's familiar and wrong instead of what's new and right.

Mindbody relaxation increases the chances of success of all weight loss programs by treating the underlying cause of overeating which is tension. A successful weight loss program includes several components, including exercise, portion control, and healthy choices. But they're all hard to do when you're tense. When you're tense, you know what you're supposed to do, but it's easy to get side-tracked. When you're relaxed it's easier to make the right choices.

> **"Mindbody relaxation increases the chances of success of all weight loss programs because it treats the underlying cause of overeating."**

Consider the case of Jackie, a customer service rep who came to me because she wanted to deal with her stress. All day Jackie had to listen to the complaints of her clients, and on top of that she put up with a difficult boss. Jackie was a single mother who absolutely loved her son, but he required a lot of energy. At the end of the day Jackie was so exhausted that she would go through a bag of cookies just to settle down before going to sleep. Then the next day she would get up and do the same thing all over again.

Jackie wanted to lose weight. She was disciplined in other areas of her life, but when it came to controlling her urges for overeating she felt like she was fighting a losing battle. The key to Jackie's success was not to eat less. Then how would she deal with her stress and tension? I pointed out to Jackie that the key was to learn how to let go of her tension. Then her eating would be about eating, instead of being about relaxing or rewarding herself.

Jackie took my advice and made mindbody relaxation part of her life. She practiced every day. When I saw her a month later she said she could feel the difference. She was more relaxed at the end of the day. Little things didn't bother her during the day, and it was even easier to deal with her boss.

Jackie didn't feel she had to come home and comfort herself with a bag of cookies. She could come home and let go of her tension with a relaxation session. When I saw her a month after that, she had already started to lose weight. But even more important she felt better. She looked better and even her son commented that she was more relaxed.

You will see results quickly. If you relax for thirty to forty minutes a day, within a month you will feel more relaxed and have fewer urges to overeat. Within three to four months you will see a maintained difference in your eating habits and in your weight. Within a year your new eating habits will be part of your life.

It really works. You just have to practice relaxation every day. You can't reduce your tension and keep it low if you don't relax every day. You can't lose weight and keep it off if you don't make relaxation part of your life. It's a small price to pay. A new life, a new waistline, less tension – and all you have to do is relax for thirty to forty minutes a day.

"You get a new life, a new waistline, less tension – and all you have to do is relax for thirty to forty minutes a day."

16.
ENJOY BETTER RELATIONSHIPS

Everyone wants a good relationship. The world feels like a better place when you're in one. The problem is that all relationships start out beautifully, but then at least half of them fail within a few years. What role does tension play, and how can relaxation help?

Resentments and fears combine to destroy most relationships. If you don't know how to let go of resentments, you'll build layer upon layer of resentments until that's all you see. Fears undermine relationships from the beginning, because they make it hard to let down your guard and communicate. **Tension makes it hard to show affection and hard to receive it.** It makes it hard to love and be loved. Everyone knows that communication is essential for good relationships, but communication is exactly what you can't do when you're tense. So you stick to the superficial stuff and watch your relationship wither.

Dr. John Gottman is one of the world authorities on relationships. He can predict with 90 percent accuracy whether a marriage will fail or succeed after studying it for only five minutes!

Dr. Gottman has boiled what makes relationships work down to a few basic principles.[40]

This chapter looks at those principles from the point of view of tension. How does tension hurt relationships, and how does letting go of tension improve them? There's nothing new about these principles. You've heard most of them before. What is new is seeing how important tension is to all of them.

"The heart that loves is forever young."[42]

The Principles of Healthy Relationships

Healthy couples express their affection for each other every day. You may be surprised to know that healthy couples have occasional negative thoughts about each other. Some days you'll wake up and wonder what you ever saw in your mate. That's normal. Healthy couples make it easier to let go of those negative feelings by expressing their affection for each other every day. That way, when occasional negative thoughts do arise, they don't overwhelm your positive feelings.

When you receive affection every day and give it every day, it's easier to shrug off the little annoyances. The simple act of saying, "I love you," or "You look good today," makes a world of difference in the strength of your relationship. Later, when one of you is a little short with the other, or when one of you speaks in a certain tone of voice, it's easier to assume that it's because the other is tired, instead of assuming that it's because they're angry or because they don't love you. Part of being romantic is celebrating the small positive things in your relationship. Without those little expressions of affection, it's easy for little annoyances to build up into major resentments.

What role does tension play? Tension makes it hard for you to let go of the little resentments so that you can express your affection. Tension makes you dwell on the past and relive the negatives until you turn them into big resentments. Relaxation prevents little resentments from building up and poisoning your relationship. It prevents stupid little things from getting in the way of you saying the important things, like "I love you."

"Relaxation prevents little resentments from building up and poisoning your relationship."

Healthy couples acknowledge each other's invitations for affection. Every day, your partner makes small overtures for your affection. They offer bits of conversation or enter your physical space hoping for a hug. It's one of the ways that healthy couples strengthen the bond between them. Healthy couples make and respond to those gentle invitations more often than unhealthy couples. But that's hard to do when you're tense. Those gentle invitations are usually silly bits of conversation. Nothing important. In fact they're not even meant to be important. They're just an opening for something more important – a hug or a kiss. But when you're tense you tend to take those gentle invitations literally, and you end up criticizing them or ignoring them. You can't see past their smallness to what they really mean – "Please give me a hug."

Healthy couples ask for each other's opinion and follow it when it has merit. It's one of the ways that healthy couples show respect for each other. When you're tense, it's hard to be open to another opinion. You have one way of seeing things and one way of doing things – your way. Even if it's the wrong way, you stick with what you know, partly out of stubbornness and partly out of the fact that you don't have room in your mind for anything else.

Healthy couples don't allow arguments to escalate. Healthy couples argue just as much as unhealthy ones. But they argue differently. They don't allow their arguments to get out of control. They make conciliatory gestures, like saying, "I'm sorry," or "Let's try that again." Have you ever sat down hoping to have a nice civilized conversation, only to watch it turn into a fight?

When you're tense you bring in resentments from your day and let them contaminate your conversation. You're really angry about something that happened earlier, but you take it out on the person you love because you didn't let it go earlier. If you're not aware of the underlying causes of your tension, when you get home you don't even know why you're angry, you just know that you are. When you're relaxed, it's easier to leave that stuff at the office. You have fewer buttons to push.

Healthy couples ask each other what they're thinking, and take the time to listen. All couples fear growing apart, but they do little to prevent it. Knowing what your partner is thinking and feeling is one of the best protections against growing apart. You both will grow and change over time. That's inevitable.

Healthy relationships can handle differences. What they can't handle is silence – which is another way of saying that communication is essential for healthy relationships. But communicating is what you can't do when you're tense. When you're tense, you talk about the superficial stuff, and with each conversation your relationship grows more superficial.

Being in the moment helps you hear what your partner is saying. This is especially true for the subtle messages they send out in the early stages of a disagreement. When differences of opinion are still small, most people don't explicitly say there is something wrong. Instead, they send out indirect signals that are hard to read. Those signals are especially hard to read when you're tense and when your mind is somewhere else. But you ignore those subtle signs at your own peril. They may be nothing.

But then again they may be a sign that you're starting to move in different directions. When you're relaxed and in the moment it's easier to hear those subtle clues and catch little problems before they become big ones.

Healthy couples focus on the positives instead of the negatives. The best summary of these qualities is that healthy couples focus on the positives instead of the negatives. Healthy couples realize that nobody is perfect, and that no relationship is perfect. They begin by finding the right partner, and then work at appreciating what they have. That's different than settling for a relationship. Settling implies not finding the right partner in the first place, and then ignoring their negative traits without focusing on their positives. Settling is an act of apathy. Healthy relationships are based on mutually appreciating the positives.

Unhealthy couples look for the right partner and then quickly become dissatisfied with what they have because they focus on the negatives. Then they look for someone better, where better usually means different. Once they've settled into their new relationship, they discover that they have to make a new set of compromises, and then they eventually become dissatisfied with that relationship and move on to the next one.

Tension makes it hard to focus on the positives because when you're tense you feel dissatisfied with almost everything. You feel uncomfortable in your own skin, which makes it hard to appreciate anything else. Relaxation helps you feel satisfied with what you have by helping you feel comfortable with yourself.

> **"Ask yourself this: will more resentments, more fears, and more tension improve your relationship?"**

If you're still not sure about the importance of relaxation in your relationship, ask yourself this: will more resentments, more fears, and more tension improve your relationship?

The Signs of Unhealthy Relationships

This section looks at the flip side of healthy relationships. How does tension make good relationships bad and unhealthy relationships worse?

Unhealthy couples begin arguments harshly. Unhealthy couples start with what's wrong and why it's the other person's fault. Research has shown that if a disagreement begins in that tone, it will end negatively 96 percent of the time, even if the couple tries to "make nice" in between.[41]

What role does tension play? When you're tense, it's hard to hold your resentments back. You want to get stuff off your chest, and you're not exactly thinking about how the other person feels. Suppose you've had a bad day, or you've had to deal with difficult people, and you come home and want to tell it to someone. If your partner doesn't respond exactly the way you had hoped, it's easy to take out your frustrations on them. You forget the real cause of your tension, and instead you focus on the current little irritation.

When you're relaxed, it's easier to see the big picture. Take a deep breath and focus on what's really bothering you. Or even better, spend twenty minutes when you come home to relax so that you can let go of your resentments and enjoy your evening.

When you do have a disagreement, start with the positives. Begin with how much your relationship means to you and how much you enjoy it. Don't just say the words – mean them. Remember that you're holding something fragile in your hands when you begin an argument. Begin with the positives not only to reassure your partner, but also to remind yourself of the big picture. That's easier to do when you're relaxed.

Unhealthy couples engage in a death spiral of criticism, contempt, defensiveness, and withdrawal. The death spiral begins with criticism. Unhealthy couples don't offer neutral suggestions. They go beyond the problem at hand and criticize their partner's character. It sounds like "Could you please clean up this mess? You're so lazy." The more tense you are, the more your criticism can escalate into contempt. "You're such a slob." Contempt is the most deadly part of this sequence because it involves name-calling, and name-calling implies that you are disgusted with your partner. No one can have a rational conversation with you if they think you're disgusted with them.

Once contempt is out of the bag, defensiveness soon follows. Your partner responds with the fact that it's not their fault, it's yours. "I'll clean it up eventually, but you're the one who started dinner late." The final step is withdrawal. One of you feels overwhelmed and stops communicating. The less one of you communicates, the more the other becomes agitated and contemptuous. Can you see the role that tension plays in this story? It is all fueled by resentments, fears, and tension.

Finally, unhealthy couples turn away from conciliatory gestures. Even if your relationship has all the unhealthy qualities listed above, it can still survive if it has one positive quality. Healthy couples turn toward each other after an argument. They offer conciliatory gestures to repair hurt feelings. Studies have shown that couples who turn toward each other after an argument, even if they have all the other unhealthy qualities, still have an 84 percent chance of remaining happily married after six years.[42]

Letting go of tension makes it easier to offer conciliatory gestures and easier to accept them. When you're relaxed, it's easier to remember this isn't about who gets in the last word. It's about being happy in your relationship. Of course that makes sense, and of course name-calling isn't good for a relationship. It's just that common sense doesn't come easily when you're tense.

Consider the case of Norman and Margaret. He's a vice president of a bank and a recovering alcoholic. She's a consultant with a busy practice. They have two teenage children. Norman was in recovery for two years and doing well, but Margaret was still resentful of all the things he had put her through. She was justifiably resentful. Norman had been a Jekyll and Hyde when he was drinking. He had embarrassed Margaret and had been rude to her. But these resentments were now getting in the way of their mutual recovery. She and Norman had been going to couples counseling for the last two years but they had made little progress. During our sessions, Margaret would sit with her arms crossed and correct every statement that Norman made.

One day, I asked Margaret what it would take for her to begin to let go of her resentments. She said she was resentful that Norman had the luxury of going to rehab and taking time to focus on himself when she had to hold the family together. I suggested that it was Margaret's turn to take care of herself. I encouraged her to put some time aside every day to relax. Norman and the children would have to take up the slack, or they would have to change their expectations.

Their recovery had to be mutual. Both Margaret and Norman had to feel better about their lives if this was going to work. This was not just about Norman stopping drinking. Margaret took my suggestion and began to relax every day. After a few months she felt a little better and started noticing that she was more tolerant toward her husband and her children. After a while the barriers that had built up over the years started to come down, and they started making progress as a couple.

Effective Communication

All effective communication is win-win. Both people have to feel that they're getting something positive from communication if it's going to work. There is no win-lose communication in a relationship. If you want to be heard and influence your partner, they will only agree to listen if they feel there is something in it for them, and if they are being treated with respect. Effective communication doesn't sound like "Let me tell you why you're wrong." If the other person has to lose, they'll make sure that you don't get to win either. Relationships are either win-win or lose-lose.

But when you're tense, it's hard to think in terms of win-win. You tend to see your choices as all or none. You think that if you agree with the other person you'll be a doormat, and if you disagree you will inevitably have an argument.

Healthy couples don't have to agree all the time. You can disagree on issues without attacking the other person. You can offer suggestions without name-calling. But you will only do it when you're relaxed. That's when it's easier to speak with compassion and listen with understanding. That's when you can acknowledge what the other person is saying and stick to the issues. It's never easy. But it's a lot harder when you're tense.

"Tension makes it hard to love and be loved."

17.
REDUCE ANXIETY AND SEIZE THE DAY

Anxiety or worry is one of the common causes of unhappiness. People are anxious about the future, what happened in the past, or what other people think about them. The basic causes of anxiety are fear, not being in the moment, and focusing on things that you can control.

But how do you eliminate anxiety? You can't stop thinking about the future. If you did that you couldn't plan for the future. The way to eliminate anxiety is by focusing on the things that you can control, and focusing on the moment instead of dwelling on the past or the future.

Anxiety can become a habit. The more anxious you are, the more you find things to be anxious about. You can get to the point where your first response when you're tense is to worry about what you can't do, instead of focusing on the things you can do. The more you worry about the things you can't change, the greater your chance of failure. Anxiety becomes self-fulfilling. Relaxation can help you break that habit.

How to Let Go of Anxiety

You let go of anxiety with the same three steps that you use to let go of tension and change your life.

- Identify the underlying causes of your anxiety.
- Let go of your tension so that you can make room for change.
- Replace your anxiety with something positive.

A relaxation session helps you with all three steps. You practice letting go of your anxiety and being in the moment so that you can be in the moment during the rest of the day. You practice focusing on the things that you can control so that you can focus on the things that you can control during the rest of the day. You practice enjoying the moment instead of feeling anxious.

Being in the moment is not the same as living in the present. "Live in the present" is commonly given advice that's impossible to follow literally. If you always lived in the present, you could never plan for the future. But there is no paradox in living in the moment. You can live in the moment and still plan for the future, as long as you are fully present in what you do. If you are going to plan, give yourself permission to plan, and don't think about all the other things you have to do. When you spend time in the moment, you become more efficient.

You let go of one thing by focusing on something else. If you have been unable to let go of your anxiety, it's because you didn't have anything to substitute for it as you were letting go. It's hard to stop feeling anxious by just telling yourself that you should feel less anxious. You need something to reach for as you're letting go of your anxiety. Mindbody relaxation gives you that something to reach for. You let go of your tension by focusing on your body and breathing, which are real and exist in the moment.

You let go of your anxiety and tension at the physical level. You relax your mind by relaxing your body, and you relax your body by becoming grounded, balanced, loose, and centered. Doing that releases you from the grip of anxiety and tension. It is as simple and profound as that.

The Medical Evidence

Mindbody relaxation reduces anxiety and panic attacks. A study at the University of Massachusetts took twenty-two patients who suffered from generalized anxiety or panic disorder and taught them how to relax. After six weeks, twenty of the twenty-two participants said they felt significantly more relaxed. The benefits were long lasting. Three months later, those patients who continued to practice relaxation continued to feel more relaxed and happy.[43]

Seize the Day

How do you seize the day? You seize the day by living in the day, instead of reliving yesterday. You seize the day by letting go of your resentments and fears so that you can be free to seize it.

Most people remember the importance of seizing the day only after some tragedy. That's when they remember to tell the ones they love how much they love them and to let go of petty resentments. That's when they remember to live in the moment and let go of the past. But then they quickly forget the importance of that lesson until the next event or tragedy comes along. The idea that life is best lived in the moment is surely one of the most frequently forgotten and rediscovered ideas in history. This day will never come again.

"Seize the day by living in the day instead of reliving yesterday."

The ability to seize the day and enjoy the moment is the hall-mark of a happy life. When people dream of what they'll do when they retire, they dream of living in the moment. They dream of not being in a rush and doing things they want to do. But then they turn around and forget to enjoy the rest of that day as if living in the moment is a luxury they can postpone until later.

In the moment is the only place where you can feel content and happy. When you're not in the moment, even the most perfect day is hard to enjoy. When you're in the moment, the little things are so much sweeter. It's where you're meant to live your life.

Tom is a high-ranking military officer. He has sacrificed a lot to get to his position. But when I saw Tom he was wondering if it was all worth it. His body was in constant pain from all the punishment it had taken over the years, and he was drinking more to deal with the pain. As I took his story, he told me of all the places he'd been to and all the things he had done, and I told him how impressed I was with his accomplishments. Tom looked away and was silent for a long time. I looked away too because I felt awkward intruding on his personal moment.

When I looked back, tears were streaming down his face. He apologized the way men do when they've been crying, and he reached for a tissue. When he was able to talk again, he said that he thought about all the times he had missed with his family: birthdays, anniversaries, special events. Even when he was there, he wasn't really there. He had been a good provider for his family, but now that he had achieved everything he had always wanted, he wondered if it was worth the price. He wondered if he should have slowed down and enjoyed the little things with his family.

This man with a granite jaw, whom other men would walk through a brick wall for, was crying over the simple moments he had missed with his family. He had been so busy achieving in his life that he forgot to pay attention to what really mattered.

I've often wondered why something as important as how to be happy and live in the moment is rarely taught in school. It seems that the further we go in school the more specialized information we learn. But the really important stuff, like what will make us happy, is hardly ever taught. Why is that?

"I went to the woods because I wished to live deliberately ... and see if I could not learn what it had to teach, and not, when I came to die, discover that I had not lived."[44]
– Henry David Thoreau (1817–1862)

"In the moment is the only place where you can feel happy and content."

18.
DEVELOP UNDERSTANDING, COMPASSION, AND TOLERANCE

Understanding, compassion, and tolerance are the basis of all human relationships. All major religions are founded on them. They are the basis of all personal, business, and international relationships. They bring out the best in people and help people bring out the best in each other. But understanding, compassion, and tolerance are hard to express when people are tense. In this chapter you will learn how letting go of tension helps support the foundation of all human relationships.

Understanding

If you want to understand people, you have to understand how they deal with tension. Most people spend more time feeling anxious and resentful than they do feeling joyful or happy. People are driven by tension. There are other factors that you have to understand about people of course, but if you don't understand how they deal with tension they'll surprise you most of the time.

Because when people are tense they tend to do what's familiar and wrong. Most of the bad behavior you encounter during the day is due to the fact that people are up to their eyeballs in tension.

Tension distorts people's behavior because they have accumulated layers of tension. When people don't know how to let go of their tension, they add more layers of tension to the pile every day. By the time you meet them, it's all they can do to get through the day without snapping. You say something or do something that seems innocuous, but without knowing it, you've triggered some deep layer of tension in them, and suddenly they snap. That alone explains many of the bad interactions you have.

> **"If you don't understand how people deal with tension, they'll surprise you because when people are tense they tend to do what's familiar and wrong."**

Relaxation helps you understand people because it helps you understand yourself. When you understand the underlying causes of your tension, you also understand them in others. When you understand how you behave when you're tense, you also understand how other people behave. Learning to relax will help you avoid conflicts and repair relationships.

The Oracle of Delphi was counsel to the ancient world for over a thousand years. Over its entrance were written the words – "Know thy self."

Compassion

"The essence of the Buddha's teachings can be found in two sayings. If possible, you should help others. If that is not possible, at least you should do no harm."[45] – The Dalai Lama

The Buddha's message is about compassion and tolerance. Compassion is about being kind to others. Tolerance is about doing no harm. Here harm means not only physical harm but also psychological and emotional harm. Both qualities, compassion and tolerance, are difficult to show when you're tense. When you're tense, you become rigid with intolerance, and fears and resentments get in the way of your compassion.

Compassion is how we connect with other people. Compassion is the basis of all healthy relationships because it's a gift that you give both to the other person and to yourself. Every child knows that the best way to have a positive and lasting relationship with them is through compassion. Every adult can remember someone whose compassion had a pivotal impact on their life. Even a little compassion can sometimes turn an adversary around. You have as many reasons for compassion as you have relationships in your life.

> **"When you're full of resentments, there isn't room in your heart for anything else, including liking yourself."**

Compassion is also the best way to like yourself. It's a purely selfish reason for being compassionate, but it's hard to like yourself when you're full of resentments. When you're full of resentments, there isn't room in your heart for anything else, including liking yourself. But when you are compassionate, you create a circle that quickly comes back to you. The best reason to do the right thing is that it's the right thing for you.

Compassion is the key to letting go of tension. When you have compassion in your heart, it's easier to let go of the layers of tension that you have accumulated. When you go out into the world with compassion, you prevent new layers of tension from forming. Without compassion you will spend every relaxation session letting go of the tension that you accumulated from the day before.

How do you develop compassion? It's one thing to say that compassion is good for you. But how do you develop it? Mindbody relaxation is especially helpful here. It shows you how to cultivate compassion. We are all born with the capacity for compassion. As a species we couldn't exist without compassion. Therefore you don't have to learn how to be compassionate. Instead, you have to let go of the obstacles that are getting in the way of your compassion. Mindbody relaxation helps you let go of your fears and resentments so that your natural compassion will come out. When your mind is clear of tension and your heart is free of resentments and fears, you will find the compassion within you.

"My religion is kindness."[46]
– *The Dalai Lama*

"In this world
Hate never yet dispelled hate.
Only love dispels hate.
This is the law,
Ancient and inexhaustible."[47]
– *The Buddha*

Tolerance

Compassion is always the first choice when interacting with another being, but unfortunately compassion isn't always possible. Every day you come across angry and insensitive people who are under extraordinary stress. Sometimes the best you can do is understand that the other person is full of tension and let go of their behavior so that you don't carry it with you and become resentful.

Sometimes the best you can do is tolerate people's behavior. That doesn't mean you agree with it or condone it. It just means that you realize you can't control everything and everyone around you, and becoming angry over someone else's behavior is a waste of your energy. Tolerance is always preferable to resentments because tolerance is cheaper than aggression. And if there is a chance that you can help someone change, it's more likely to happen in a climate of tolerance.

Sometimes even your capacity for tolerance will be tested. Some people will push you to your limit. You've tried to set healthy boundaries, you've tried to be tolerant, but they just don't get it. They're so full of tension and anger themselves that they can't appreciate your tolerance. In their case, the best thing you can do is avoid them, because that too is a form of tolerance.

"When we talk about how we should develop tolerance… we should not misunderstand this to mean that we should just meekly accept whatever is done against us. [Sometimes] the best, the wisest course, might be to simply run away – run miles away!"[48]
– The Dalai Lama

Let Go of Deep Resentments

An important part of tolerance and compassion is letting go of resentments. Everyone has deep resentments, and everyone has fantasies of revenge. The question is not whether you have resentments, but what you will do about them. Will you hold on to them until the other person has apologized? Will you dwell on your fantasies of revenge until you poison yourself? Or will you let them go?

The point of this section is to remind you that you don't have to let go of your resentments because it's the noble thing to do. You don't even have to forgive the other person if you don't want to. Let go of your resentments because it's good for you. Let them go, because if you don't, you will continue to be a victim, and the other person will continue to win. Why do you know that it's good for your friends to let go of their resentments, but you continue to hold on to yours?

There is a wonderful piece of advice that summarizes why you should let go of your resentments. "You will not be punished for your anger – you will be punished by your anger."[49]

**"You will not be punished for your anger –
you will be punished by your anger."**

How do you let go of resentments? First, you have to understand that you can't permanently let go of resentments. You can't expect to never be bothered by resentments again. You can't erase the past, and you can't pretend it never happened. But you can learn to quickly let go of the resentments that you feel when you think about the past, which is the next best thing.

Letting go of resentments is not the same as denial. Denial is an exhausting strategy for dealing with the past because it takes energy to deny reality. Of course bad things have happened. Of course your resentments hurt; that's why you're still thinking about them. But if you try to deal with your resentments by denying them, you'll give them more room to grow. If you try to deal with your resentments by not feeling anything, the price you'll pay is that you'll become emotionally dead inside, and you won't feel any joy either.

So how do you let go of resentments? You let them go in the same way that you let go of other forms of tension, by admitting that you are resentful, and then relaxing your body. Name your resentments as a source of tension, relax your body, and return to the moment. It's the opposite of denial.

Don't be in a rush to let go of deep resentments. The difference between deep resentments and other resentments is that deep resentments have deep roots. They crop up when you least expect them. They are so connected to your subconscious that they can be triggered by almost anything. You'll be minding your own business, when all of a sudden one of them will jump up and make you just as angry today as it did years ago.

Here's the important point. If you rush to let it go, if you think it's silly that you're still resentful, you'll overlook its deep roots and never completely let it go. You've been cultivating your deep resentments for years. It will take at least a few years to let them go. But the more you practice letting them go, the more your resentments will lose their emotional charge.

When you find yourself struggling to let go of a resentment, stop and give yourself a choice. You can dwell on your resentment or save your energy. You can poison yourself or move on. You can let the other person win or take control of your life. Which would you rather do?

"Holding on to anger is like grasping a hot coal with the intent of throwing it at someone else; you are the one getting burned." [50]
– The Buddha

"Be kind when possible. If that's not possible, at least do no harm."

19.
OVERCOME DEPRESSION
AND ADDICTION

This chapter looks at how mindbody relaxation prevents and treats depression and addiction, and how it helps treat post-traumatic stress disorder.

Ask your doctor or therapist if mindbody relaxation is right for you. Relaxation can complement the work you do with your doctor or therapist, but it doesn't eliminate the need for their guidance.

Depression

Ten to thirty percent of people will suffer from at least one episode of depression in their life. The medical definition of depression is at least one of the following: low mood, low energy, low sense of enjoyment, or high anxiety, for at least two months. But the best nonmedical description is that depression feels like lack of vitality.

There are three basic causes of depression.

1. A family history of depression, which makes you
   genetically predisposed.
2. Abusing drugs or alcohol, which are brain depressants.
3. Feeling that you're trapped in a box that you can't
   escape from.

How Tension Can Cause Depression

If you feel you are trapped in a box, such as a job that you don't like or an unhealthy relationship that won't change, you'll struggle against that box until you eventually become exhausted and depressed.[51]

> **"Tension can lead to depression by making you feel that you're trapped in a box that you can't escape from."**

The box you struggle in can be external, like a job or a relationship, or it can be internal, like poor self-esteem. Below are some examples of how you can make yourself depressed by living inside a box of tension.

Poor self-esteem can cause depression. If you believe that you never get a break in life, then you're trapped in a box of your own making. Your belief can become a self-fulfilling prophecy, because if you behave as if you never get a break, then people will begin to respond to you that way, and sure enough you won't get a break. The more you live in that box, the more tense you'll become, the more energy you'll consume, and the more depressed you'll feel.

Resentments can cause depression. Resentments trap you in a box because they make you feel uncomfortable in your surroundings. With each new resentment and with every new fault that you find in the world, you make your zone of comfort smaller and your world less enjoyable. If you have enough resentments and if you spend your time dwelling on the things that you can't change, you will eventually become mentally exhausted and depressed.

Never being satisfied with what you have can cause depression. If you're always chasing after something more than what you have, you're saying that you're in a box you want to get out of. A little of that can be motivating. But if you set your standards so high that you can't realistically achieve them, then you're setting yourself up for disappointment, and you've built a box that you can't get out of. Of course everybody thinks they'll stop when they get what they really want. But many people develop a habit of chasing after things, and by the time they get what they had initially wanted they find it hard to break that habit. If you continue to struggle in that box, after a while you'll feel let down and depressed.

Trying to live up to someone's expectations can cause depression. Right off the bat when you try to live up to someone's expectations, you've created a box that you don't want to live in. You force yourself to live in it out of a sense of duty or obligation, but you know that you'd be happier doing something else.

The most common example is trying to live up to your parents' expectations. The mistake I see a lot of people make is that they take their parents' expectations too literally. They think their parents want them to grow up to have a specific job or to make a specific amount of money. Most parents just want their children to grow up and be happy. For many people that's a liberating realization.

James was extremely clever in school. His parents wanted him to grow up and be a doctor, and because he was so bright, it was easy for him to follow that path. He got married to a wonderful wife who was proud of his accomplishments. But James had a passion for cooking, and his goal was to retire early from medicine and set up a quaint little neighborhood restaurant. His dream was that he would get to know the locals, and his food would be the sanctuary they would turn to at the end of the day.

When his wife heard of his ambition, she said she couldn't understand it. She didn't think it was a dignified retirement for a doctor, and she told him that if he persisted in pursuing it she would have to leave him. When I met him he was sobbing as he told me his story. Now I'm not saying there's an easy answer to this problem. But I am saying that because he felt trapped by other people's expectations, James was profoundly depressed. When I met him he was so depressed that ultimately he was no good to anybody, including himself or his wife.

How Letting Go of Tension Treats Depression

Mindbody relaxation prevents and treats depression by helping you escape the traps you make for yourself. A relaxation session is a model of self-change. First, a relaxation session makes you aware of how you trap yourself, then it helps you let go of your tension so that you can be open to change, and finally it helps you create healthier beliefs.

During a relaxation session you become aware of how you trap yourself by hearing the negative messages that you repeat to yourself. Do you tell yourself that you never get a break? Do you ask yourself "why me?" when something goes wrong? Do you dwell on your resentments? Do you tell yourself to always hurry up because you're afraid that people will think you're lazy? Those are some of the common messages people repeat to themselves that cause depression. But it's easier to hear them when you're relaxed.

Once you become aware of how you trap yourself, mind-body relaxation helps you let go of those traps, by helping you let go of your tension. During a relaxation session, you practice letting go of the past. You practice letting go of your resentments and fears so that you can make room for change.

Finally, mindbody relaxation helps you create a healthier way of life that reduces the chances you will become depressed in the future. You practice living in the moment and letting go of the past so that you can incorporate that way of living into your daily life. Later in the day, when the thought creeps in that you're a failure or that you never get a break in life, it's easier to let go of that thought because you practiced letting it go earlier.

You practice letting go of the past, so that you can focus your energy on the things that you can change, which increases your chance of success and makes you more optimistic for the future. The more you practice that way of living the easier it will to be to incorporate in to your life.

The same way that repeating negative messages can become a negative self-fulfilling prophecy, repeating positive techniques can also transform your life.

How Relaxation Prevents Depression

Mindbody relaxation prevents depression from occurring in a few ways. First, mindbody relaxation builds your self-esteem so that you don't believe the destructive criticism that you may have heard in the past.

Second, mindbody relaxation prevents little resentments and fears from building up and turning into major ones that can trap you or draw you into the past.

Finally, mindbody relaxation helps you practice letting go of the past and living in the moment, which restores your optimism and reduces your risk of future depression.

Once you've been depressed, it's common to worry that there's another episode of depression waiting for you just around the corner. Depression is so devastating and painful that after one episode, you're worried it will happen again. That worry can become another box that can trap you. You can spend your energy living in the past instead of enjoying the present. Mindbody relaxation helps you let go of the past, which reduces your risk of recurrence.

The Medical Evidence

Mindbody relaxation can reduce the risk of recurrence of depression by 50 percent. One study looked at fifty-five patients who had recently recovered from depression. They were randomly divided into two groups. One group received regular medical follow-up, while the other group was also taught how to relax. Both groups were followed for sixty weeks.

Seventy-eight percent of the non-relaxation group had another episode of depression during the next sixty weeks, while only 36 percent of the relaxation group had another episode of depression during the same time.[52] The simple act of relaxation reduced the risk of a recurrence of depression by half.

Addiction

An addiction is any behavior that you have difficulty controlling and that you continue to do, even though it's had negative consequences to your life. The classic addiction is alcoholism. But the definition applies equally well to drug addiction, gambling addiction, eating disorders, and sexual addiction. Addiction crosses all socioeconomic boundaries. Ten percent of any population meets the criteria for a drug or alcohol addiction, which means that addiction is more common than diabetes.

The First Rule of Recovery

You don't recover from addiction by simply stopping using. You recover from addiction by creating a new life where it is easier to not use. I have worked in the field of addiction medicine all my professional life, and I believe this is the most important thing that patients and their families need to understand. If addicts don't create a new life, all the factors that brought them to their addiction will eventually catch up with them again. Recovery isn't about stopping – it's about changing your life.

How Tension Contributes to Addiction

Why do addicts use drugs or alcohol in the first place? They use them to escape, relax, or reward themselves. In other words, they use them to deal with tension. Everyone needs to escape, relax, and reward themselves. Those are essential skills in the pursuit of happiness. But addicts don't know how to do them without using.

The most important thing that addicts need to change is they need to discover healthier ways to escape, relax, and reward themselves. If they don't learn those healthy skills, the world will be too painful for them, and they will eventually relapse just to escape.

> **"Addicts use drugs or alcohol to relax, escape, or reward themselves. In other words, they use them to deal with tension."**

Even if recovering addicts manage to stop using for a while, if they don't learn how to relax, they will relapse eventually, because their anxiety, tension, and uncomfortable feelings will continue to build.

The tension that addicts want to escape is usually internal. For example, poor self-esteem can create tension that addicts want to escape, because poor self-esteem makes people feel uncomfortable in their own skin. Fear can also create tension that addicts want to escape. Not being in the moment and having a racing mind also create tension that addicts want to escape.

Donald had a stressful job and a young family of three children. He loved his family, but sometimes he couldn't face the idea of going home directly after work. He needed to unwind. So he would buy a bottle of vodka on his way home. Then he would park his car a block from home and sit in his car and drink the bottle before facing the rest of his evening. His wife was upset when he came home drunk. His children were getting short-changed, because he didn't spend as much time with them. Donald knew all these things, and he had tried many times to stop, but he kept on relapsing.

Donald couldn't expect to succeed by just stopping drinking. He needed to replace what alcohol was giving him. He needed to find new and healthier ways to escape the stress in his life. Relaxation could be that escape. Or relaxation could be part of that escape. One thing is certain, if the only thing he did was stop drinking, eventually he would go back to what was familiar and what was making both him and his family unhappy.

How Relaxation Prevents and Treats Addiction

- Relaxation improves your self-esteem so that you have less reason to turn to drugs and alcohol.
- You let go of your resentments, fears, emotional pain, and the underlying tension that leads to addiction.
- You learn a coping skill that you can use to escape, relax, and reward yourself.

- Relaxation reduces your risk of relapse because when you're relaxed it's easier to do what's new and right, instead of repeating old habits that are familiar and wrong.

I know relaxation will help. I have treated thousands of patients. Many of them have told me that relaxation has changed their life.

There is only one reason why people don't relax. They think they're too busy to relax. It goes something like this: "I know it makes sense, but I've got so many other things I have to do."

Ask yourself how much time you spend on your addiction. If you add up all the time it takes to get your drug, use it, deal with its consequences, hide the evidence, and plan your next relapse, relaxing for twenty to forty minutes a day is a bargain. If you relax for forty minutes a day on weekdays, and one hour a day on weekends, I promise you will save time, be happier, and do better in your recovery.

Relapse Prevention

It's one thing to stop using drugs or alcohol. It's another thing to stay clean and sober and to avoid relapsing. In this section you'll learn about relapse prevention and how mindbody relaxation can help.

Relapse is a process, it's not an event. In order to understand relapse prevention you have to understand there are stages of relapse. Relapse starts weeks or even months before the event of physical relapse. There are three stages to relapse. [55]

- Emotional relapse
- Mental relapse
- Physical relapse

In emotional relapse, you're not thinking about using. But your emotions and behaviors are setting you up for a possible relapse in the future. The signs of emotional relapse are:

- Anxiety
- Intolerance
- Anger
- Defensiveness
- Mood swings
- Isolation
- Not asking for help
- Not going to meetings
- Poor eating habits
- Poor sleep habits

Because you're not consciously thinking about using, it's hard to believe that you are moving toward relapse. Therefore a big part of emotional relapse is denial. When someone suggests that you're at risk for relapse you become defensive.

By learning the early warning signs of relapse it's easier to catch yourself quickly. In the later stages of relapse the pull of addiction gets stronger and the sequence of events move faster.

Early relapse prevention means recognizing what you're doing wrong and changing your behavior. Recognize that you're isolating and remind yourself to ask for help. Recognize that you're anxious and practice relaxation. Recognize that your sleep and eating habits are slipping and practice self-care.

Practice self-care. The most important thing you can do to prevent relapse at this stage is take better care of yourself. Think about why you use. You use drugs or alcohol to escape, relax, or reward yourself. Therefore you relapse when you don't take care of yourself and you create situations that are mentally and emotionally draining that make you want to escape.

For example, if you don't take care of yourself and eat poorly or have poor sleep habits, you'll feel exhausted and want to escape. If you don't let go of your resentments and fears through relaxation, they will build to the point where you'll feel uncomfortable in your own skin. If you don't ask for help, you'll feel isolated.

How do you go from emotional relapse to mental relapse? If you don't change your behaviors and you live too long in emotional relapse, you'll become increasingly uncomfortable or exhausted, and when you're exhausted you will want to escape. You will begin to think about using as a way of escaping, which will move you into mental relapse. That's why self-care is so important.

In mental relapse there's a war going on in your mind. Part of you wants to use, but part of you doesn't. In the early phase of mental relapse you're just idly thinking about using. But in the later phase you're definitely *thinking* about using. The signs of mental relapse are:

- Thinking about people, places, and things you used with
- Glamorizing your past use
- Lying
- Hanging out with old using friends
- Fantasizing about using
- Thinking about relapsing
- Planning your relapse around other people's schedules

It gets harder to make the right choices as the pull of addiction gets stronger. Here are some of the techniques that you can use to deal with mental urges during mental relapse.

Play the tape through. When you think about using, the fantasy is that you'll be able to control your use this time. You'll just have one drink. But play the tape through. One drink usually leads to more drinks. You'll wake up the next day feeling disappointed in yourself. You may not be able to stop the next day. Your relationships will begin to suffer. You'll get caught in the same vicious cycle. When you play that tape through to its logical conclusion, using doesn't seem so appealing. It's easier to play the tape through when you sit down and relax. Otherwise your mind is so full of noise that you can't hear the faint voice of reason.

A common thought during mental relapse is that you can get away with using, because no one will know if you relapse. Perhaps your spouse is away for the weekend, or you're away on a trip. That's when your addiction will try to convince you that you don't have a big problem, and that you're really doing your recovery to please your spouse or your work. Play the tape through. Remind yourself of the negative consequences you've already suffered, and the potential consequences that lie waiting for you if you relapse again. If you could control your use, you would have done it by now.

Tell someone that you're having urges to use. Call a friend, a support, or someone in recovery. Share with them what you're going through. The magic of sharing is that the minute you start to talk about what you're thinking and feeling, your urges begin to disappear. They don't seem quite as big and you don't feel as alone. All of that is easier to do when you're relaxed and not driven by fear or exhaustion.

Distract yourself. When you think about using, do something to occupy yourself. Go to a meeting. Get up and go for a walk. Have a relaxation session. If you just sit there with your urge and don't do anything, you'll give your mental relapse room to grow.

Wait for 30 minutes. Most urges usually last less than 15 to 30 minutes. When you're in an urge, it feels like an eternity. But if you can keep yourself busy and do the things you're supposed to do, it'll go quickly.

Do your recovery one day at a time. Be in the moment. Don't think about whether you can stay abstinent forever. That's a paralyzing thought. It's overwhelming even for people who've been in recovery a long time. But if you are in the moment, you don't sabotage yourself by thinking too far ahead.

One day at a time, means that you match your goals to your emotional strength. When you feel strong and you're motivated to not use, then tell yourself that you won't use for the next week or the next month. But when you're struggling and having lots of urges, and those times will happen often, tell yourself that you won't use for today or for the next 30 minutes. Do your recovery in bite-sized chunks.

The final stage of relapse is physical relapse. Once you start thinking about relapse, if you don't use some of the techniques mentioned above, it doesn't take long to go from there to physical relapse. Driving to the liquor store. Driving to your dealer.

It's hard to stop the process of relapse at that point. That's not where you should focus your efforts in recovery, because relapse prevention at that point is hard work. That is the difference between abstinence and recovery. If you recognize the early warning signs of relapse, and make mindbody relaxation part of your life, you'll be able to catch yourself before it's too late.

The Medical Evidence

One study looked at 126 individuals who abused alcohol. After practicing a relaxation technique for two years, 40 percent reported that they had stopping drinking. After three years, 60 percent reported they had stopped drinking.[53]

Another article reviewed twenty-four research studies that looked at the benefits of relaxation in preventing and treating substance abuse. It concluded that relaxation is effective in preventing substance abuse and effective in treating substance abuse. It also concluded that relaxation helps develop long-term improvements in well-being, self-esteem, and psychological health.[54]

Relaxation may mimic the calming effects of alcohol and tranquilizers. Alcohol and tranquilizers work by increasing a neurotransmitter called GABA (gamma-aminobutyric acid), which is the main calming neurotransmitter in the brain. There is evidence that relaxation also increases the amount of GABA in the brain, which may explain its calming effects.[55]

Post-Traumatic Stress Disorder

Post-traumatic stress disorder is a condition that sometimes develops after a person has been exposed to severe trauma such as violence or abuse that they are powerless to stop. Survivors of trauma often respond to the trauma by mentally shutting down and not living in the moment as a way of dealing with their pain. It's an effective strategy in the short term but doesn't work well in the long run.

Those suppressed emotions of fear and resentment have to come out somehow, and they often come out in the form of anger, anxiety, depression, nightmares, and rage.

It's been my experience that some people develop post-traumatic stress disorder, not after one overwhelming trauma, but after many accumulated smaller traumas. If you don't know how to let go of tension, many repeated traumas can have the same effect as one big trauma. This is corroborated by the fact that not everyone who is exposed to major trauma goes on to develop post-traumatic stress disorder. This is especially true for adults. Adults who go on to develop post-traumatic stress disorder are usually the ones who had painful or traumatic childhoods. Therefore, I prefer to think of post-traumatic stress as accumulated traumatic stress disorder.

Part of the treatment of accumulated traumatic stress disorder is teaching survivors grounding techniques similar to those used in mindbody relaxation. They're taught how to become grounded and centered so that they can connect with the moment and prevent their anxiety from overwhelming them.

The long-term treatment of accumulated traumatic stress disorder also involves mindbody relaxation techniques. Survivors are encouraged to gradually let go of their tension so that they can reconnect with their emotions and become whole again.

Trauma survivors are understandably anxious when they first try to relax because they are reluctant to give up control. But relaxation isn't about giving up control. It is about regaining control by letting go of the tension that has been running their lives. Although most people prefer to relax with their eyes closed, trauma survivors usually prefer to relax with their eyes open in the beginning.

"Mindbody relaxation prevents and treats depression and addiction, and helps with the treatment of post-traumatic stress disorder."

20.
How Relaxation Complements Psychotherapy

Both mindbody relaxation and psychotherapy work in similar ways. They both help you improve your self-esteem, build better relationships, deal with past issues, and find happiness. In this chapter you'll learn how mindbody relaxation can complement psychotherapy.

Ask your doctor or therapist if mindbody relaxation is right for you. Although relaxation can complement the work you do with your doctor or therapist it does not eliminate the need for their guidance.

How Distorted Beliefs Cause Unhappiness

One of the most common forms of psychotherapy used today is cognitive behavioral therapy (CBT).[56] Cognitive therapy is based on the idea that distorted beliefs make you unhappy and keep you stuck in your unhappiness.

For example, if you believe that you never get a break in life, that distorted belief will obviously make you unhappy. But it will also keep you stuck in your unhappiness because it can become a self-fulfilling prophecy.

If you believe that you never get a break, you will begin to behave that way, and eventually people will respond to you that way. Your distorted belief will keep you stuck in your unhappiness by sabotaging your ability to change.

Consider another example. Suppose you've always been told that you'll never amount to anything. If you hear that often enough, after a while you may begin to believe it, and that can then become a distorted belief that can affect the way you approach the world. Or maybe you've been told that the only way you'll ever amount to anything is if you're always serious, hardworking, and maybe even a little unhappy.

It only takes a few distorted beliefs to change the course of your life. What may have started out as a small misconception can end up having a huge impact on your life. When people say they have "issues," they usually mean that they have distorted beliefs.

"Mindbody relaxation works in a similar way to cognitive therapy."

Cognitive therapy helps you recognize your distorted beliefs, let them go, and learn healthier beliefs in their place. Mindbody relaxation works in a similar way. It is a model for self-change. Mindbody relaxation complements psychotherapy by helping you identify the tension that makes you unhappy, let it go, and learn a healthier way of living.

Common Distorted Beliefs

These are the common distorted beliefs that trap most people:[57]

- All-or-None Thinking: "I have to do something almost perfectly, because anything less will be a failure." "Change is difficult because it means I have to change everything I'm used to."
- Fortunetelling: "I know this won't work. Nothing ever works for me."
- Disqualifying the Positives: "I never get a break in life. My life feels like one negative after another."
- Catastrophizing: "Now that this bad thing has happened, my whole day has been ruined. I'll be playing catch-up for the rest of the day."
- Mind Reading: "I know they don't like me."
- Self-Labeling: "You don't have to be nice to me. I know I screwed up. I'm a loser."
- Disqualifying the Present: "I'll be able to relax later. But first I have to rush to finish this."

A distorted belief is absolute and irreversible. It is absolute if you see things as all or none. For example, you either have to be perfect or you'll be a failure. Your whole day has to go well or the smallest thing can ruin it. If you see things that way, you'll probably end up choosing the negative. A distorted belief is irreversible if you think that things can't change. For example, you'll never get a break.

Relaxation Helps You Recognize Your Distorted Beliefs

Cognitive therapy helps you identify your distorted beliefs by encouraging you to keep a "thought record" of your day. After each time you feel uncomfortable, you're encouraged to write down what you were thinking, and identify the underlying distorted beliefs behind your thoughts. For example, were you engaged in all-or-none thinking or disqualifying the positives? Keeping a thought record helps you identify your distorted beliefs more quickly in the future.

Mindbody relaxation helps you identify your distorted beliefs, because most distorted beliefs are caused by tension. When you're angry, your thoughts become absolute because you have only one way of seeing things – your way. When you're afraid, your thoughts become irreversible because you're paralyzed by fear. When you worry about the future, you're engaged in fortune-telling. When you dwell on your resentments, you disqualify the positives. Tension underlies most distorted beliefs.

An important distorted belief is the belief that dwelling on the cause of your unhappiness will make you happier. It's not one of the standard distorted beliefs of cognitive therapy, but it's one that many people lapse into. It is what makes you replay events from the past again and again. You tell yourself that you want to understand what happened so that you won't let it happen again. But how many times do you have to go over the same thing? You end up reliving your resentments and fears, and building more tension, instead of letting it go.

All-or-none thinking not only makes you unhappy, it also keeps you stuck in your unhappiness because it makes it difficult to imagine change. When you're tense, you think that any change implies a big change, therefore you resist it. You can't see the small steps, therefore you're not open to change.

Relaxation helps you identify your distorted beliefs in the same way it helps you identify your tension – by being a reflection of your life. Whatever makes you tense and is an obstacle to happiness in your daily life will also be an obstacle to your relaxation. But during the day it's hard to recognize your distorted beliefs because everything is happening so quickly. When you're relaxed, it's easier to step back and see how you make yourself tense and how you get in the way of your happiness.

The most profound insight of psychotherapy is that people often recreate the painful experiences of their childhood in their adult life. The distorted beliefs that are planted during childhood become the causes of unhappiness in adulthood. People who were overly criticized as children often become perfectionists and overly critical as adults. People who didn't receive love as children often end up in loveless or cold relationships.

If you were overly criticized as a child, your distorted belief probably is that you see the world as all or none. You probably also tend to disqualify the positives. If you didn't receive love as a child, your distorted belief probably is that you engage in self-labeling. Relaxation helps you see your underlying tension so that you can let it go and learn something better in its place.

Laura's father was a prominent lawyer who was loving but critical. Laura is nice at work, but she is surprisingly critical of her son. She wants him to be the best he can be and to take advantage of the opportunities he has been given. But Laura's criticism is having the reverse effect. It is starting to become destructive instead of inspiring change. It has affected her son's self-esteem to the point where his grades are getting worse. What started out with the best of intentions is having the opposite effect.

Laura's distorted belief is her all-or-none thinking. Her son has to be the top in his class or he will have wasted his life. She learned that belief from her father, and now she's teaching it to her son. When her son doesn't follow her beliefs and when he isn't a perfectionist, Laura is overly critical.

I encouraged Laura to start her evening with a relaxation session before she deals with her family issues. When she's relaxed, she'll have a better perspective on whether she needs to push so hard or whether there is a better way.

Let Go of Your Distorted Beliefs

Cognitive therapy helps you let go of your distorted beliefs by encouraging you to keep a thought record. Mindbody relaxation works in the same way. You practice letting go of your tension and distorted beliefs by naming them, so that you can recognize them in the future. Beliefs are not irreversible. The more quickly you can recognize them, the more quickly you can let them go.

There is a parable about the importance of letting go of unhappiness that comes from the Buddha. Suppose, he said, a man is wounded by a poison arrow, and his friends rush him to a doctor. But suppose the man won't let the doctor take out the arrow until he learns who shot him. Suppose the man wants to know the person's name, where he was from, and why he shot him. The man would probably die before he could get the answers to his questions. But he could live if he stopped dwelling on why he was hurt and let go of what was hurting him.

Cultivate Healthy Beliefs

Mindbody relaxation not only helps you let go of your unhealthy beliefs, it also helps you replace them with healthier beliefs. During a relaxation session you practice letting go of your resentments instead of catastrophizing the situation. You practice letting go of your fears instead of seeing things as all-or-none. You practice enjoying the moment instead of disqualifying the positives. You practice changing your life.

Cognitive therapy and mindbody relaxation are not based

on the fantasy that you will be happy if you just think happy thoughts. The opposite of disqualifying the positives is not thinking random happy thoughts. The opposite of disqualifying the positives is being in the moment and not dwelling on past resentments.

The more you practice your new beliefs the easier it will be to incorporate them into your life. The more you incorporate them into your life, the more your life will improve.

Cognitive Therapy for Caretakers

Caretakers are the people who take care of everybody else and usually put themselves last. They are often mothers, but they are also fathers, older siblings, and children of aging parents. They do everything that's expected of them. They feel responsible for everything and everybody, and at the end of the day when they have nothing left to give they crash from exhaustion.

Caretakers don't know how to take care of themselves because they've been told that it's selfish. It's one of the recurring themes in my practice. The underlying distorted belief of being a caretaker is that taking care of yourself is selfish. The underlying tension is fear. Caretakers are afraid of being criticized or being called selfish. The way out of that box is to understand that self-care is not the same as selfishness.

Selfishness involves taking more than you need. But caretakers usually take less than they need, which is why they end up becoming exhausted. Self-care involves taking some time just for you so that you can enjoy your life. If you don't take care of yourself, you won't have anything left for anyone else. You have to put some time aside every day just for you, if you want to be happy and be able to take care of others. Relaxation can be that time. It is the practice of self-care.

"Self-care is not the same as selfishness."

Caretakers have difficulty practicing self-care because they have a hard time saying no in a healthy and constructive way. The distorted belief is that if you say no, you will hurt the other person's feeling and things will never be the same between the two of you. Or if you say no, the other person will have an explosive reaction, because that's what you've experienced in the past. The underlying tension, again, is fear.

There is also the fear that you won't know how to set healthy boundaries. Once you start to say no, how will you make sure that you don't get carried away and start saying no to everything? How will you know where to draw the line so that you don't end up becoming selfish?

Mindbody relaxation helps you find that healthy balance. When you let go of your fears and resentments, you aren't motivated by distorted beliefs and you aren't reacting to old scenarios; therefore it's easier to find the balance of self-care.

Caretakers often come from turbulent families. If you're a caretaker, you probably grew up in a family that was unreliable, therefore as an adult you try to control the external aspects of your life. The distorted belief is that you will feel relaxed and happy when everyone else is happy or when everything is in its place. But doing that puts the responsibility for your happiness on external factors. You will only feel relaxed is if you take responsibility for becoming relaxed yourself. Fixing your external world will only go so far. Beyond that you will exhaust yourself if you try to fix your outside world but ignore your inside world.

The only two alternatives they see are either continuing to be a caretaker or running away and abandoning their relationship. If they continue caretaking, they are so caught up in their role that they find it hard to imagine healthy intermediate ways of escaping or relaxing. Because they see the world as all-or-none, any escape that they imagine is usually grand and impractical. Therefore they trap themselves even further by hoping for an escape that they know they can't take.

If you're going to start taking care of yourself, it's important that you lay the groundwork by preparing the people around you. Prepare them for the change so that taking an escape won't backfire and make you feel even more guilty. Tell the people in your life that you are getting exhausted and that you need some time just for yourself so that you'll have more energy. Tell them that you'd appreciate their support. All they have to do is give you a little time for yourself.

Start small with something you can do in a few hours, and expect that it will feel awkward at first. But you are creating some breathing room in that tight little box that you're living in. And with time it will start to have benefits in all aspects of your life.

Psychotherapy for Anger Management

Anger destroys relationships, careers, and personal health. It is one of the most destructive emotions.

Anger management is based on the following principles:

- Identify the feelings behind your anger, and learn how to express your feelings constructively.
- Recognize your anger in the early stages before it causes problems.
- Let go of your anger so that it doesn't build up over time.

Mindbody relaxation complements all aspects of anger management. Mindbody relaxation helps you recognize your anger so that you can catch it early. You practice recognizing the tension, resentments, and fears that lead to anger by becoming aware of how they distract you when you try to relax.

When you are distracted by a resentment or fear, name your tension as the first step in letting it go. Say to yourself, "That's a resentment. Let it go." When you name your tension, you shift from being controlled by your tension to controlling it.

Mindbody relaxation also works by helping you communicate your feelings better. When you're relaxed it's easier to find the right words, and to see the situation from the other person's point of view.

A relaxation session is a safe laboratory in which you practice letting go of your tension and resentments. You practice letting go of your anger during a relaxation session so that you can let it go during the rest of the day. The techniques that you use to let go of your resentments and return to the moment during a relaxation session are the techniques you will use in the rest of your life.

The Medical Evidence

Numerous studies have noted the similarities between cognitive behavioral therapy and mindbody relaxation. An article in the *American Journal of Psychiatry* noted that mindbody relaxation is "an effective cognitive technique for the development of self-awareness."[58]

A review of the psychotherapy literature said that mindbody relaxation techniques "may, in some cases, be compatible with, and effective in, promoting the aims of psychotherapy – for example, cognitive and behavioral change."[59]

Cognitive Therapy and Mindbody Relaxation

Mindbody relaxation and cognitive therapy both focus on letting go of the past, instead of exploring the past. Cognitive behavioral therapy represents a fundamental shift in the way psychotherapy is done. Psychotherapy used to be based on the idea that exploring the past was the most important part of change. The result was that people would sometimes spend years in psychotherapy, exploring their childhood, and make little progress.

Cognitive therapy changed that by recognizing that exploring the past is only part of change. You need to understand the past in order to understand how it affects your present. But dwelling on the past beyond that point doesn't help, if anything it makes you more tense and more unhappy. The most undervalued part of change is letting go of your distorted beliefs so that you can create room for change.

This is how relaxation complements psychotherapy. It creates room for change. If you don't let go of your tension, you will continue to repeat what's familiar and wrong instead of trying what's new and right. Relaxation helps you identify your distorted beliefs, let them go, and practice new beliefs so that you can begin to enjoy your new life.

"Mindbody relaxation complements psychotherapy by helping you identify the tension that makes you unhappy, let it go, and learn a healthier way of living."

21.

RELIEVE PHYSICAL PAIN

There are two components to pain. When you're physically hurt, you experience both physical and psychological pain. The psychological component of pain is the fear or anticipation of more pain. In many cases, the psychological component of pain causes more discomfort than the actual physical pain.[60]

Believe it or not, morphine works by relieving the psychological component of pain. It does not reduce physical pain. If you've ever had morphine you know what I mean. The pain is still there, but you're so relaxed that it doesn't hurt as much. By reducing the psychological component of pain, morphine reduces the total pain you experience.

Mindbody relaxation works on the same principle as morphine. Morphine releases endorphins, which are your body's own pain relievers. Relaxation has also been shown to release endorphins.[61] But mindbody relaxation also reduces the underlying cause of pain by relaxing the muscles and ligaments that are in pain.

Mindbody relaxation relieves pain in two ways.

1. Mindbody relaxation relaxes the muscles and ligaments that are in pain, which reduces the physical component of pain.
2. Mindbody relaxation releases endorphins, which reduce the psychological component of pain.

If you relax for twenty minutes twice a day, you'll release endorphins twice a day and have that much less need for pain medication.

How Mindbody Relaxation Relieves Physical Pain

Consult your physician before trying this. Your doctor will want to rule out if there are any serious causes for your pain. Once your doctor gives the go-ahead, start by trying this on a minor ache. Remember that mindbody relaxation should be used as a complement to standard medical therapy and not on its own.

Begin by relaxing for at least twenty minutes. Then select a minor ache or pain that you would like to reduce. Focus on the physical sensation of the pain. Don't try to ignore the pain or eliminate it. That will only increase your resentment of the pain and the psychological component of pain. Feel around the edge of the ache, where it's easiest not to get overwhelmed. Focus on how the pain feels around the edges. Don't think about the pain – feel it. As you do this, keep breathing from your abdomen.

Now imagine the area warming up and your muscles and ligaments relaxing and melting and releasing the tension. Some people find it helpful to imagine a white light filling up the painful area and gradually replacing the pain.

As you focus on your pain, you will probably tense up other areas of your body. Therefore you'll have to periodically remind yourself to relax the three main areas of your body: your core muscles, chest muscles, and face. Once you've relaxed your body, return to focusing on the physical sensation of the pain.

Within fifteen to twenty minutes, you'll feel the pain gradually diminish and sometimes even spontaneously disappear. The first time it happens, you'll be utterly amazed. But it really works. Of course, it's easier to do with minor aches, but the principle applies to most kinds of pain.

Next is some of the medical evidence that mindbody relaxation is effective in relieving pain. Mindbody relaxation has been medically proven to relieve both acute and chronic pain. What's amazing is how effective it is in relieving chronic pain. Chronic pain is traditionally hard to treat, because pain creates a pain cycle. The more your pain lingers, the more psychological pain it creates.

> **"Mindbody relaxation has been medically proven to relieve acute and chronic pain."**

The Medical Evidence

Relaxation relieves chronic pain. One pain study looked at 180 chronic pain patients. They all received standard medical treatment; in addition, half of the group also received a ten-week course in mindbody relaxation. The results were dramatic. Almost immediately, the relaxation group started to need less pain medication. After fifteen months, they had significantly less pain. Not only did the relaxation group suffer less pain, but because they had less pain they also suffered less depression and anxiety than the non-relaxation group.[62]

Relaxation reduces the pain and disability of chronic low-back pain. One study looked at thirty-six patients with chronic low-back pain. They were randomly divided into two groups. One group received intensive physical therapy, while the other received an eight-week course in mindbody relaxation without any physical therapy.

Both groups were followed for six months. At the end of the six months, the relaxation group had significantly improved in all areas. Their mobility and lack of pain were similar to the group that received intensive physical therapy, even though the relaxation group received no physical therapy.[63]

Relaxation reduces the symptoms of fibromyalgia. Fibromyalgia is a chronic illness that is characterized by pain, fatigue, and sleep disturbance, and sometimes occurs together with chronic fatigue syndrome. Fibromyalgia has traditionally been difficult to treat because those symptoms set up a cycle where one symptom triggers the others, and all have to be treated simultaneously, otherwise the patient will make little progress. One study looked at seventy-seven fibromyalgia patients and treated them with a ten-week course in mindbody relaxation. Amazingly, 51 percent of the patients experienced moderate to marked improvement in their symptoms.[64] That is virtually unheard of in most treatments of fibromyalgia.

Relaxation can help treat cancer pain. A large-scale review of twenty-eight pain studies concluded that mindbody relaxation is an effective supplement to conventional medicine for the treatment of the following kinds of pain:[65]

- Headaches
- Chronic low-back pain
- Cancer pain symptoms

How Mindbody Relaxation Treats and Prevents Migraines

One day Robert walked into my office complaining of blinding migraines. He had seen a number of doctors before seeing me and each one had treated him with narcotics. But Robert was concerned that he might become addicted to them, and he wanted to look at alternatives. I thoroughly checked him out to see if there were any other causes for his migraines, and then I spent the next few sessions teaching him how to relax. At the end he thanked me and said he was going to give it a try.

Now this is the spooky part. Six years later, to the very day, he returned. He walked into my office with a big smile on his face and told me that he had been practicing relaxation every day for the last six years, and he was virtually free of migraines. The results were almost immediate. Friends who knew him well, and knew how much he suffered from migraines, had jokingly suggested that I must have been a witch doctor. Robert had taught the technique to his niece who also suffered from migraines, and she also found it effective. He had come back six years later to say thank you.

Relaxation doesn't usually eliminate migraines, but it can reduce the frequency and severity of most migraines.

There is a specific technique to relieving headaches and migraines. Begin by relaxing your body and becoming grounded, balanced, loose, and centered as you do in standard mindbody relaxation. Many migraines are either triggered or made worse by tension in the face and eyes. It's known, for example, that migraines are reduced by botox injections into the forehead that relax the forehead muscles. Therefore the main focus of this technique is to relax your face and eye muscles.

Close your eyes and imagine that your surroundings are completely black. Imagine that you're looking at a black screen, and that you're in a completely black room. Take care not to squint because that increases eye tension. When your eyes are tense, you'll see lights or colors in your field of vision. When your eyes are relaxed, your vision will be pure black. It's a little hard to describe, but most people get the hang of it pretty quickly.

This technique is slightly different from the one described in Chapter 4 *"Use Your Body to Relax Your Mind."* In that chapter one of the techniques for becoming centered was to imagine your body filling up with white light. Here the focus is on relaxing your eye and face muscles. Therefore it's more important that you imagine looking at a black screen. You will still become centered in this technique, but it will happen by you focusing on being grounded, balanced, and loose.

This technique works like biofeedback. Your eyes will instantly tell you if your eye muscles are tense because you'll see lights or colors in your field of vision. With that feedback, you'll be able to let go of your face and eye tension quickly.

How Tension Causes Headaches and Backaches

Headaches and backaches are the most common kinds of pain for which patients seek medical help. Most are caused by tension. Tension headaches and backaches cost billions of dollars each year in medical costs and time off work. Any improvement in how we treat them would be a major step forward.

"Most headaches and backaches are due to tension."

Let's suppose you have a stressful job, but you don't know how to relax. The tension has to go somewhere. If you're one of those people who stores their tension in their back, your muscles will begin to tighten up. One day your back may be so tight that the slightest jarring movement will produce a sudden backache.

Once your back starts to hurt, you'll subconsciously react by changing your posture to compensate, which will put more strain on your back. If you continue to build tension, it can eventually turn into a vicious cycle that can turn into chronic back pain.

Consider another example. Suppose you have a car accident and hurt your back or develop whiplash. Each time you think about the accident you get angry and frustrated. The more frustrated you get, the more tension you build. The more tension you build, the more pain you feel, which can turn into a vicious cycle that can end up as chronic neck pain.

At least 90 percent of headaches are muscle tension headaches. Tension in your jaw, eyes, and neck can result in a headache. The more your head hurts, the more likely you are to tighten your jaw and neck, which causes more pain and can lead to another vicious cycle.

How does tension cause muscle pain? When your muscles are tight, they release chemicals called cytokines that cause pain. The pain is meant as a warning signal to tell you that you should slow down and change what you're doing. But if you ignore those warnings, your muscles will become more tense, and eventually your simple headache or backache can turn into a chronic pain.

Mindbody relaxation helps you heal quickly after an injury or accident. Backaches that are due to an injury or accident can be difficult to treat because the underlying tension isn't usually treated. Patients go through rounds of expensive investigations, take stronger pain killers, and sometimes still don't get better.

Some people won't make much progress until they let go of their frustration and resentment about the accident. I'm not saying that's the most important part of recovery after an accident. But teaching patients mindbody relaxation can reduce the physical and psychological components of pain, preventing backaches from turning into chronic pain, and helping patients heal faster.

"Mindbody relaxation reduces the physical and psychological components of pain and helps you heal faster."

22.
IMPROVE YOUR CREATIVITY

It's easier to think outside the box when you're relaxed. Newton had his big idea sitting under a tree. (I know it's just a myth, but I like the message.) Creativity happens when you're relaxed.

Genius may be 90 percent perspiration and 10 percent inspiration, but the inspiration happens when you're relaxed and free of tension. When you're tense, you tend to think more of the same and do more of the same.

Have you ever had this experience? You want to solve a problem, and you think long and hard about it, but you don't get anywhere. Then you take a break, and all of a sudden the answer pops into your head. Why? Because when you are thinking hard, you are doing the groundwork and perspiration of creativity, but then when you relax, you're able to see the big picture and get the inspiration of creativity.

The hard work of creativity is also easier to do when you're relaxed because when you're in the moment, you focus your energy on the task at hand, which makes you more efficient. When you're tense, you mistake action for motion, and do a lot of little things that don't amount to much.

"When you're tense, you mistake action for motion, and do a lot of little things that don't amount to much."

Creative writing courses teach people to get their creative juices flowing by writing free-form. Just sit down and write. Don't stop to correct your spelling. Don't worry about punctuation. Just write as fast as you can. Why? Because when you write like that, you don't get in your way. The voices of self-doubt and criticism that are the death of creativity are temporarily silenced. Later, you can go back and tidy up the writing. But that's the easy part. That's just applying rules. The real moment of inspiration, the feeling of being touched by fire, your unique voice that can't be taught and that has nothing to do with rules, can come only when you're unafraid and in the moment.

One of the basic rules of creativity is to be yourself and find your own style. It's also one of the hardest rules to follow. How do you be yourself? You are yourself when you are free of tension. Fear and anger are the obstacles to being yourself. When you're tense and in a rush, you create what's safe and ordinary.

The goal of artists is to tap into their deepest emotions, to shed their fears, and to see things from a fresh perspective. Sometimes they sacrifice themselves on the altar of drugs and alcohol to get a little closer to that goal. But you can achieve those goals automatically by learning how to relax.

Natalie is an author and psychotherapist who has written a few books. When I met her, she had been working on her last book for five years and had made little progress. She was terrified that she had writer's block. In our first session, I asked Natalie to forget about writing and to tell me about the rest of her life.

Natalie's second book had been quite successful, and she had dreams of becoming a full-time writer. But the rest of her life was in chaos. Natalie's husband suffered from depression and had lost four jobs during the course of their marriage. Natalie was afraid that he was relying on her success. They spent every second weekend visiting her parents, who were getting older, and her father, who drank a little too much, was suffering from early Alzheimer's. Natalie wanted to know why she couldn't just bury herself in her work like she used to.

I reminded Natalie that she was in survival mode. She was focused on her emergencies. She didn't have any energy left for the luxury of creative thinking.

Relaxation can't make Natalie's problems go away. But it can give her a little breathing room and reenergize her so that she can deal with her problems. It can also help her distinguish the things she can change from the things she can't change. It seemed to me that the biggest obstacle to Natalie's creativity was that she was focused on the things she couldn't change. She was drained because she felt responsible for everything. She wanted to know what more she could do, when the answer was probably nothing. And just as important, nobody else thought she could do more. Her husband, her children, and her parents realistically knew she couldn't do more. None of them wanted her to get sick.

I suggested that maybe Natalie could take a little time for herself and give herself a break. I suggested that she try relaxing every day. It would help her step back and see her problems with greater clarity. It would also create a little calm in her hectic schedule so that she wasn't always in crisis mode. It would also rejuvenate her so that writing would be fun again.

"It's easier to think outside the box when you're relaxed."

23.
RAISE THE LEVEL OF YOUR GAME

Anyone familiar with football history is familiar with the story of Joe Montana and Super Bowl XXIII. With three minutes left in the game, Joe Montana and the San Francisco 49ers were trailing the Cincinnati Bengals by three points. All of a sudden Joe looked into the stands and said, "Hey look, there's John Candy."

Montana was so in the moment that he could spot the actor out of 75,000 fans. The team settled down and in the next few minutes marched 92 yards up the field to win the Super Bowl. Joe Montana turned the game around because he was relaxed and in the moment. He was in the zone.

When you're in the moment, time slows down and you can see everything around you. You don't waste your energy on what just happened or what might happen. You focus your energy on what is happening, which increases your chances of success.

"When you're in the moment, you don't waste your energy on what just happened or what might happen. You focus your energy on what is happening."

The Fundamentals of Athletic Success

Dr. Joel Kirsch of the American Sports Institute spent five years studying the qualities that determine athletic success. He calls them the eight fundamentals of athletic mastery (FAMs): concentration, relaxation, attitude, flexibility, balance, power, rhythm, and instinct.[66] The first four are mental qualities, and the last four are physical qualities.

- Concentration – The ability to focus on your task.
- Relaxation – Lack of tension so that you can be open to what's happening around you.
- Attitude – A combination of patience, perseverance, and positivity.
- Flexibility – The ability to adapt positively to changing situations.
- Balance – Stability so that you can't be knocked over either physically or mentally.
- Power – The ability to apply the appropriate amount of force at the right time, as quickly as possible.
- Rhythm – Movements that are graceful and efficient and that seem to come from within.
- Instinct – The spark that drives you.

How Relaxation Improves Athletic Success

Four of the fundamentals of athletic mastery are improved with relaxation. Concentration and relaxation are obviously improved with relaxation. Attitude, the third quality, is also improved by relaxation because relaxation improves your self-esteem so that you can be patient and positive. Flexibility, the fourth quality, is improved because when you are tense you do what is familiar and wrong, which makes you inflexible. When you're relaxed, you can adapt to changing situations. All aspects of your mental game are improved by relaxation.

Peak performance is a mental thing. At the top level of sports, everyone is in excellent physical condition. Therefore games are won or lost, not because of a physical edge, but because of a mental edge. The person or team who is the most relaxed and most in the moment usually wins.

This is most evident during playoffs when athletes are expected to raise the level of their game. Michael Irvin, three-time Super Bowl champion of the Dallas Cowboys, says you can't run faster or jump higher during the playoffs. The only way you can raise the level of your game is by being more focused.[67]

One of the obstacles athletes have to overcome during a game is the time they spend waiting between points. Trevor Moawad, director of mental conditioning at the sports-training facility IMG Academies gives the example of a tennis match. In a typical two-hour tennis match, only about forty minutes are spent playing the game.[68] That leaves an hour and twenty minutes when you're alone with your thoughts, which gives you plenty of time to talk yourself *out* of the game.

When you're tense, the conversation with yourself is probably going to be negative. When you're relaxed, you don't get in your own way. Mindbody relaxation helps you not talk yourself out of a game.

"Mindbody relaxation helps you not talk yourself out of a game."

How Relaxation Helps Outside the Game

Relaxation also helps athletes deal with the stresses they face outside of the game. That's when self-doubt and self-destructive behaviors can creep in and undo the hard work of training.

Athletes live in a world of extremes. On the one hand, they have more freedom than most people. On the other hand, they're more under a microscope than most people. They are constantly being watched by their coaches, fans, and the league. It's the kind of situation that makes people want to look for an escape. When you're relaxed, it's easier to deal with those pressures.

"You'll be amazed – amazed – at how fresh you feel, when you forget everything in your life except what you're doing right now."[69]
– Bill Cowher, head coach of the Super Bowl XL Champion Pittsburgh Steelers

"Four of the fundamentals of athletic mastery are improved with relaxation – concentration, relaxation, attitude, and flexibility."

24.
REDUCE TENSION AT WORK

Tension and stress cost American businesses $300 billion a year.[70] Tension reduces productivity and innovation . It increases health costs, accidents, absenteeism, and employee turnover. Reducing tension makes good business sense.

This chapter will look at what management can do to reduce tension. The focus is on management because there's little that an individual can do to reduce the structural causes of tension at work. In a dysfunctional workplace, the best an employee can do is reduce their own tension so that they don't take it home with them.

Here are four examples of how tension hurts business, based on the four basic causes of tension: not being in the moment, resentments, fears, and trying to control things you can't control.

Not Being in the Moment and Reduced Productivity

People are most productive when they maintain a balance between being in the moment and being focused on the long-term goals of their work. The paradox is that when people are too focused on the short-term goals and work too fast, they become less efficient. When they're focused on just finishing their job, they can't step back and see the big picture, which ends up causing mistakes. Mistakes don't usually happen because people are incompetent. They usually happen because people are too tense to see the big picture.

The Dirty Secret of Resentments

Resentments are the biggest cause of tension at work and one of the biggest challenges for management. People respond to resentments at work in the same way that they do at home. They dwell on their resentments and hatch fantasies of revenge. Listen to people complain about their work. Rarely do they complain about *what* they do, instead they almost always complain about *who* they work with. It takes only a few disruptive people to create an atmosphere of resentment in a workgroup.

Resentments reduce productivity, not just because of the time lost, but because of the counterproductive things people do when they are resentful. They lie and scheme and undermine each other. When management ignores conflicts, or only pretends to deal with them, the resentments don't go away. People have long memories for stuff like that. What do you do when you're resentful? Jack Welch has said that lying and lack of candor are "the biggest dirty little secret in business."[71] They are obstacles to good decision making and productivity.

> **"Resentments reduce productivity, not just because of the time lost, but because of the counterproductive things people do when they are resentful."**

Robert Sutton, professor of management science at Stanford University, has shown that leaders who tolerate "jerks" just because they are productive are practicing a false economy. "Jerks" drain the energy and effectiveness from everyone around them.[72]

I don't think managers tolerate jerks because they think that it's good for the company. They tolerate them usually because they don't know how to deal with them.

Destructive Criticism

Fear and destructive criticism have the same effect at work that they do at home. Dysfunctional managers try to control people by being shaming or dismissive. Of course, that doesn't inspire change. Only a small percentage of people work harder out of fear. Most people respond by becoming dysfunctional themselves. They outwardly agree with the need for change and then drag their heels to undermine it. A small percentage of people become critical of everybody else, and eventually the entire work environment is poisoned.

Managers who try to control things they can't possibly control are the classic micromanagers. The more they micromanage, the more people rebel, which again reduces productivity.

One of my patients, Dennis, is a sales director at a large corporation with a lot of political infighting. He was brought in as a wonder kid to turn around the sales department. But his vice-president was probably jealous and made Dennis's tenure difficult. The vice-president micromanaged Dennis and publicly criticized every mistake Dennis made.

Dennis was a hard worker who took his work home every night and most weekends. But eventually Dennis began to hate his work. He went to work every day feeling resentful. Dennis had normal blood pressure before he started his job, but in the last year his blood pressure had gone through the roof. He made jokes about it to his co-workers and circulated emails about his head exploding. Eventually the stress, the resentments, and the micromanaging all took their toll.

Now Dennis is on stress leave. His company is paying him to stay at home and do nothing. It's not getting the benefits of his expertise, and most of the changes that he was supposed to implement are on hold. How productive is that? How much responsibility does his vice-president bear?

The Cost of Tension

Tension destroys excellence and flexibility. The basic theme of these examples is that tension has the same causes at work that it does at home, and people respond to tension in the same way at work that they do at home. When people are tense, they do what's familiar and wrong instead of what's new and right. In other words, excellence and flexibility, the very qualities that business values most, are the victims of tension.

Executive Burnout

Executives are trained to multi-task, to anticipate, and to always live in the future. But sometimes they get to be so good at those skills that they forget to turn them off when they go home. The result is that they forget how to live in the moment. As they get better at their job, they get worse at enjoying their life.

"Tension is a common cause of executive burnout."

Tension is a common cause of executive burnout. I have treated many cases of executive burnout, and I can tell you that the common theme in all of them is that they had difficulty relaxing. Executives often take a longer time to recover from burnout because they are so driven that they ignore the early warning signs. They keep pushing themselves until they're absolutely exhausted. Both the treatment and prevention for executive burn-out is to teach people how to relax.

Tension affects the bottom line. Tension causes increased health costs, higher job turnover, and reduced productivity. It costs American business $300 billion a year. That's a lot of tension.

Many prominent business leaders meditate. Here are some who have been written about:

- Bill Ford, head of Ford Motors
- Bill George, CEO of Medtronic, who says, "Out of anything, it has had the greatest impact on my career."
- Alan Lafley, CEO of Proctor & Gamble
- Michael Rennie, managing partner of McKinsey, who has studied the benefits of meditation in corporations
- Robert Shapiro, CEO of Monsanto
- Michael Stephen, chairman of Aetna International
- Walter Zimmerman, energy analyst whose daily reports are followed by hundreds of institutional investors
- A former chief of MI-5, England's security agency[73]

If they can find the time to meditate, maybe you can too.

> **"Tension reduces productivity and innovation, and increases health costs, accidents, absenteeism, and employee turnover."**

CONCLUSION

Tension is the greatest preventable cause of unhappiness. Not only does tension make you unhappy, it keeps you stuck in your unhappiness by being an obstacle to change. When you're tense, you tend to do what's familiar and wrong instead of what's new and right.

Letting go of tension is the missing piece of how you change your life. It helps you recognize how you make yourself unhappy, let go of your unhealthy patterns, and relearn something better.

The foundation of all human relationships, understanding, tolerance, and compassion, are encouraged and developed through mindbody relaxation. For thousands of years, people have found peace, happiness, and good health through relaxing their body and mind.

"You must be the change you wish to see in the world."[74]
– Mahatma Mohandas Gandhi (1869–1948)

RESOURCES

Books

- Better Brains. *Scientific American.* Sept 2003.
- *Eight Weeks to Optimum Health: A Proven Program for Taking Full Advantage of Your Body's Natural Healing Power.* Andrew Weil. Ballantine Books, 1998.
- *Feeling Good.* David D. Burns. William Morrow, 1980.
- *Full Catastrophe Living.* Jon Kabat-Zin. Delta, 1990.
- *Mindfulness in Plain English.* Henepola Gunartana. Wisdom, 1991.
- *Perfect Health: The Complete Mind/Body Guide.* Deepak Chopra. Harmony, 1991.
- *The Physical and Psychological Effects of Meditation.* Michael Murphy and Steven Donovan. Institute of Noetic Sciences, 1999.
- *The Relaxation Response.* Herbert Benson and Miriam Klipper. Avon, 2000.
- *The Seven Principles for Making Marriage Work.* John M. Gottman and Nan Silver. Three Rivers Press, 1999.
- *The Six Pillars of Self-Esteem.* Nathaniel Branden. Bantam, 1994.
- *Tao Te Ching.* Lao-Tzu.
- *The Way of Zen.* Alan Watts. Vintage, 1989.

Organizations

American Institute of Stress

A not-for-profit organization established in 1978 as a clearinghouse for stress-related information. Its founding members included Hans Selye, Linus Pauling, Alvin Toffler, Bob Hope, Michael DeBakey, and Herbert Benson.

American Institute of Stress
124 Park Avenue
Yonkers, New York 10703
Tel 914-963-1200
Fax 914-965-6267
www.stress.org

The Mind/Body Medical Institute

Founded by Dr. Herbert Benson, author of *The Relaxation Response*.

The Mind/Body Medical Institute
824 Boylston St.
Chestnut Hill, MA 02467
Tel: 617-991-0102
Fax: 617-991-0112
www.mbmi.org

National Center for Complementary and Alternative Medicine

A member of the National Institutes of Health
nccam.nih.gov

The Chopra Center

A health and wellness program that uses mindbody relaxation and meditation among other things.

The Chopra Center
2013 Costa del Mar Rd.
Carlsbad, CA 92009
Tel: 760-494-1600
Fax: 760-494-1608
www.chopra.com

Dr. Dean Ornish's Program for Reversing Heart Disease

A medically corroborated program for treating heart disease that uses exercise, nutrition, and mindbody relaxation.
Preventive Medicine Research Institute
900 Bridgeway
Sausilito CA
800-775-7674
www.pmri.org

Qigong Institute

A not-for-profit organization to promote Chinese meditation, established in 1983.
Qigong Institute
561 Berkeley Avenue
Menlo Park, CA 94025
www.qigonginstitute.org

Stress Reduction Clinic

Founded by Dr. Jon Kabat-Zin, whose meditation program is used in a number of hospitals.
Center for Mindfulness in Medicine, Health Care, and Society
University of Massachusetts Medical Center
Worcester MA
508-856-2656
www.umassmed.edu/cfm

Dr. Andrew Weil
A health and wellness program that uses mindbody relaxation among other things.

Weil Foundation
PO Box 922
Vail, AZ 85641
www.drweil.com

ACKNOWLEDGMENTS

I'd like to thank my patients, who have taught me so much. I could not have written this book without the generous support and detailed suggestions of my dear friends: Bethann Colle, Michael Clark, and Suzanne Benoit.

It has been a pleasure to have worked with a number of people on this book. Editing was by Ricki Ewings and Julia Kiessling. Copy editing and indexing was by Wendy Thomas. Cover design was by Catherine McKenny. The interior layout was by Olena Sullivan. Ellen Reid was the publishing consultant. The author's photo is by Edward Gajdel.

Finally, it's an honor to thank my parents Georgia and Anthony for their love and support over the years. Thank you to everyone.

REFERENCES

1. Alan W. Watts. *The Way of Zen* (Vintage, 1957), p. 199.
2. The Dalai Lama. *How to Practice: The Way to a Meaningful Life*. Translated and edited by Jeffrey Hopkins. (Pocket Books, 2002), p. 97.
3. BCE stands for Before the Common Era and is used instead of BC. CE stands for Common Era and is used instead of AD.
4. *The Way of the Bodhisattva: A Translation of the Bodhicharyavatara* (Chapter 5) (Shambhala, 1997).
5. Lao-Tzu. *Tao-te-ching*. Bk. 1, Chapter 67.
6. Lao Tzu. *Tao-te-ching*.
7. The Dalai Lama and Howard C. Cutler. *The Art of Happiness* (Riverhead Books, 1998), pp. 13, 15.
8. Aiyoshi Kawahata. *Universal Meditation* (Heian, 1984), p. 40.
9. Traditional wisdom.
10. Dhammapada. *The Sayings of the Buddha*. Translated by Thomas Byron. (Shambhala, 1993).
11. Mark Twain. *Pudd'nhead Wilson's New Calendar*. Mark Twain Quotations, http://www.twainquotes.com/Wrinkles.html.
12. Joel and Michelle Levey. *The Fine Arts of Relaxation, Concentration and Meditation* (Wisdom, 1987).
13. Karen Armstrong. *Buddha* (Viking, 2001), p. 112.
14. M.D. Lieberman, N.I. Eisenberger, M.J. Crockett, S.M. Tom, J.H. Pfeifer, and B.M. Way. Putting feelings

into words: affect labeling disrupts amygdala activity in response to affective stimuli. *Psychol Sci* 2007 May;18(5):421–28.

15. Carlos Castaneda. *Journey to Ixtlan* (Simon and Schuster, 1972), p. 184.

16. Watts. *The Way of Zen*, p. 93.

17. Watts. *The Way of Zen*, p. 93.

18. Lawrence LeShan. *How to Meditate* (Little Brown, 1974), p. 55.

19. Zen Master Dogen. Fukanzazengi. In Jack Kornfield, editor. *Teachings of the Buddha* (Shambhala, 1996).

20. S.W. Lazar, G. Bush, R.L. Gollub, G.L. Fricchione, G. Khalsa, and H. Benson. Functional brain mapping of the relaxation response and meditation. *Neuroreport* 2000 May 15;11(7):1581–85.

21. R.J. Davidson, J. Kabat-Zinn, J. Schumacher, M. Rosenkranz, D. Muller, S.F. Santorelli, F. Urbanowski, A. Harrington, K. Bonus, and J.F. Sheridan. Alterations in brain and immune function produced by mindfulness meditation. *Psychosom Med* 2003 Jul-Aug;65(4):564–70.

22. Zen Master Dogen. Fukanzazengi.

23. Voltaire. *Philosophical Dictionary*, "Dramatic Art." 1764.

24. Attributed to William James.

25. Nathaniel Branden. *The Six Pillars of Self-Esteem* (Bantam, 1994).

26. Watts. *The Way of Zen*, p. 10.

27. E.S. Epel, E.H. Blackburn, J. Lin, F.S. Dhabhar, N.E. Adler, J.D. Morrow, and R.M. Cawthon. Accelerated telomere shortening in response to life stress. *Proc Natl Acad Sci U S A* 2004 Dec 7;101(49):17312–15.

28. Michael Murphy and Steven Donovan. *The Physical and Psychological Effects of Meditation: A review of contemporary research with a comprehensive bibliography*

1931-1996. (Institute of Noetic Sciences, 1999).

29. Norman Cousins. *Head First: The Biology of Hope* (Dutton, 1989), p. 96.

30. C. Patel, M.G. Marmot, D.J. Terry, M. Carruthers, B. Hunt, and M. Patel. Trial of relaxation in reducing coronary risk: four year follow up. *Br Med J (Clin Res Ed)* 1985 Apr 13; 290(6475):1103–6.

31. A. Castillo-Richmond, R.H. Schneider, C.N. Alexander, R. Cook, H. Myers, S. Nidich, C. Haney, M. Rainforth, and J. Salerno. Effects of Stress Reduction on Carotid Atherosclerosis in Hypertensive African Americans. *Stroke* 2000 Mar; 31(3):568–73.

32. R.J. Davidson, J. Kabat-Zinn, J. Schumacher, M. Rosenkranz, D. Muller, S.F. Santorelli, F. Urbanowski, A. Harrington, K. Bonus, and J.F. Sheridan. Alterations in brain and immune function produced by mindfulness meditation. *Psychosom Med* 2003 Jul–Aug; 65(4):564–70.

33. R.H. Schneider, C.N. Alexander, F. Staggers, M. Rainforth, J.W. Salerno, A. Hartz, S. Arndt, V.A. Barnes, and S.I. Nidich. Long-term effects of stress reduction on mortality in persons >/=55 years of age with systemic hypertension. *Am J Cardiol* 2005 May 1;95(9):1060–64.

34. R.D. Vorona, M.P. Winn, T.W. Babineau, B.P. Eng, H.R. Feldman, J.C. Ware. Overweight and obese patients in a primary care population report less sleep than patients with a normal body mass index. Arch Intern Med 2005 Jan 10;165(1):25-30.

35. Edmund Jacobson. *Progressive Relaxation: A Physiological and Clinical Investigation of Muscular States and Their Significance in Psychology and Medical Practice*, 3rd ed. (University of Chicago Press, 1974).

36. Hans Selye. *The Stress of Life* (McGraw-Hill, 1978).

37. Herbert Benson. *The Relaxation Response* (Whole Care, 1975).

38. Herbert Benson. *The Relaxation Response* (Whole Care, 2000), p. xiv.
39. Albert Schweitzer. Quoted in Norman Cousins. *Anatomy of an Illness as Perceived by the Patient* (Bantam, 1991), p. 69.
40. K. Leutwyler Ozelli. This Is Your Brain on Food. *Scientific American* 2007 Sept; 297(3): 84–85.
41. John M. Gottman and Nan Silver. *The Seven Principles for Making Marriage Work* (Three Rivers Press, 1999). John M. Gottman and Joan DeClaire. *The Relationship Cure* (Three Rivers Press, 2001).
42. Traditional proverb.
43. Gottman and Silver. *The Seven Principles for Making Marriage Work*, p. 27.
44. Gottman and Silver. *The Seven Principles for Making Marriage Work*, p. 40.
45. J. Kabat-Zinn, A.O. Massion, J. Kristeller, L.G. Peterson, K.E. Fletcher, L. Pbert, W.R. Lenderking, and S.F. Santorelli. Effectiveness of a meditation-based stress reduction program in the treatment of anxiety disorders. *Am J Psychiatry* 1992 Jul;149(7):936–43.
46. Thoreau. *Walden Pond.* "Where I Lived, and What I Lived For," 1854.
47. The Dalai Lama. *How to Practice: The Way to a Meaningful Life.* Translated and edited by Jeffrey Hopkins. (Pocket Books, 2002), p. 70.
48. The Dalai Lama with Galen Rowell. *My Tibet* (University of California Press, 1990).
49. Dhammapada. *The Sayings of the Buddha.*
50. The Dalai Lama and Howard C. Cutler. *The Art of Happiness* (Riverhead Books, 1998), p. 258.
51. Buddhist wisdom.
52. Attributed to the Buddha.

53. A.T. Beck, A.J. Rush, B.F. Shaw, and G. Emery. *Cognitive Therapy of Depression* (Guilford Press, 1979).
54. S.H. Ma and J.D. Teasdale. Mindfulness-based cognitive therapy for depression: replication and exploration of differential relapse prevention effects. *J Consult Clin Psychol* 2004 Feb; 72(1):31–40.
55. T Gorski and M Miller. *Counseling for Relapse Prevention* (Herald Publishing, 1982). T Gorski and M Miller. *Staying Sober: A Guide for Relapse Prevention* (Independence Press, 1986).
56. M. Shafil, R. Lavely, and R. Jaffe. Meditation and the Prevention of Drug Abuse. *American Journal of Psychiatry* 312 (1975): 942–45.
57. P. Gelderloos, K.G. Walton, D.W. Orme-Johnson, and C.N. Alexander. Effectiveness of the Transcendental Meditation program in preventing and treating substance misuse: a review. *Int J Addict* 1991 Mar; 26(3):293-325.
58. A.N. Elias and A.F. Wilson. Serum hormonal concentrations following transcendental meditation--potential role of gamma aminobutyric acid. *Med Hypotheses* 1995 Apr; 44(4):287–91.
59. Aaron T. Beck. *Cognitive Therapy and the Emotional Disorders* (Penguin Press, 1979).
60. David Burns. *Feeling Good* (Quill, 2000).
61. I. Kutz, J.Z. Borysenko, and H. Benson. Meditation and psychotherapy: a rationale for the integration of dynamic psychotherapy, the relaxation response, and mindfulness meditation. *Am J Psychiatry* 1985 Jan; 142(1):1–8.
62. G. Bogart. The use of meditation in psychotherapy: a review of the literature. *Am J Psychother* 1991 Jul;45(3):383–412.

63. G.S. Berns, J. Chappelow, M. Cekic, et al. Neurobiological Substrates of Dread. *Science* 5 May 2006: Vol. 312. no. 5774, p. 754–58.
64. J.L. Harte, G.H. Eifert, and R. Smith. The effects of running and meditation on beta-endorphin, corticotropin-releasing hormone and cortisol in plasma, and on mood. *Biol Psychol* 1995 Jun; 40(3):251–65.
65. J. Kabat-Zinn, L. Lipworth, and R. Burney. The clinical use of mindfulness meditation for the self-regulation of chronic pain. *J Behav Med* 1985 Jun; 8(2):163–90.
66. W.E. Mehling, K.A. Hamel, M. Acree, N. Byl, and F.M. Hecht. Randomized, controlled trial of breath therapy for patients with chronic low-back pain. *Altern Ther Health Med* 2005 Jul–Aug; 11(4):44–52.
67. K.H. Kaplan, D.L. Goldenberg, and M. Galvin-Nadeau. The impact of a meditation-based stress reduction program on fibromyalgia. *Gen Hosp Psychiatry* 1993 Sep; 15(5):284–89.
68. J.A. Astin, S.L. Shapiro, D.M. Eisenberg, and K.L. Forys. Mind-body medicine: state of the science, implications for practice. *J Am Board Fam Pract* 2003 Mar-Apr; 16(2):131–47.
69. Joel Kirsch. Teaching Methodologies: Principles and Practices for Meaningful Educational Reform, February 27, 2002. American Sports Institute, http://www.amersports.org/library/reports/5.html.
70. Michael Irvin. During an ESPN broadcast of Sunday NFL Countdown on Jan. 8, 2006.
71. Alice Park. Getting and Staying in the Zone. *Time* Jan. 16, 2006.
72. Bill Cowher. *Sports Illustrated* Jan. 30, 2006. p. 67.
73. The American Institute of Stress, http://www.stress.org/job.htm.

74. Jack Welch. *Winning* (Collins, 2005), p. 25.
75. Robert I. Sutton. *The No Asshole Rule: Building a Civilized Workplace and Surviving One That Isn't* (Warner Business Books, 2007).
76. Michelle Conlin. Meditation. *BusinessWeek* Aug. 23, 2004. Lisa Cullen. How to Get Smarter One Breath at a Time. *Time* Jan. 16, 2006. A post-modern proctoid. *The Economist* April 15, 2006. (Although I'm sure there are many women business leaders who meditate, I was unable to find any articles about them.)
77. Attributed to Mohandas Gandhi.

INDEX

self-esteem
    definition, 97–98
    improving, 101–2
    low and depression, 142
    preventing poor, 103
    and tension, 98–99
    test, 99–100
Selye, Dr. Hans, 111
sleep
    improving, 110–11
smiling
    as relaxation technique, 53–54
stress
    compared to tension, 17
Sutton, Robert, 186

T
tension
    areas in body, 38
    awareness of, 66
    as cause of depression, 142–44
    as cause of illness, 105–7
    causes, 18–19, 26
    compared to stress, 17
        and compassion, 135–36
    cost of, 188
    dwelling on, 62–63
    effects of, 10, 11, 18, 29, 30, 117
    identifying, 59–64
    layers of, 25–26
    mental, 43–45
    naming, 37, 61–63, 80
        and need for control, 23–24
        as obstacle to relaxation,
          85–86
    physical, 43–45
    recognition of, 59–60
    releasing, 67–68
tolerance, 136–37

U
understanding others, 133–34
unhappiness
    and distorted beliefs, 157–62

V
visualization technique, 41

W
weight control, 113–14, 115
Welch, Jack, 186
word
    for relaxation, 55–57, 80
work life
    reducing tension, 185–89
worry
    as cause of tension, 18

ABOUT THE AUTHOR

Dr. Melemis was born in Toronto. He has a PhD and MD from the University of Toronto and a post-doctoral fellowship from the University California at Berkeley. He has received the honor of Fellow of the Royal Society of Medicine. His medical practice specializes in mindbody relaxation, addiction medicine, and mood disorders. Some of his other interests include art, jazz, and skiing.

Contact Information

I'd like to hear your thoughts and stories about tension and relaxation. Please send them to
contact@MakeRoomForHappiness.org.

Visit the book website at
www.MakeRoomForHappiness.org.

Make Room for Happiness is published by Modern Therapies.
www.ModernTherapies.com

Printed in the United States
116592LV00002B/93/P